IN ASSOCIATION WITH

SQA

HODDER GIBSON
Model Papers
WITH ANSWERS

PLUS: Official SQA Specimen Paper & 2015 Past Paper With Answers

Higher for CfE
Human Biology

2014 Specimen Question Paper, Model Papers & 2015 Exam

Hodder Gibson Study Skills Advice – General — page 3
Hodder Gibson Study Skills Advice –
  Higher for CfE Human Biology — page 5
2014 SPECIMEN QUESTION PAPER — page 7
MODEL PAPER 1 — page 47
MODEL PAPER 2 — page 83
MODEL PAPER 3 — page 123
2015 EXAM — page 159
ANSWER SECTION — page 205

HODDER GIBSON
AN HACHETTE UK COMPANY

This book contains the official 2014 SQA Specimen Question Paper and 2015 Exam for Higher for CfE Human Biology, with associated SQA approved answers modified from the official marking instructions that accompany the paper.

In addition the book contains model papers, together with answers, plus study skills advice. These papers, some of which may include a limited number of previously published SQA questions, have been specially commissioned by Hodder Gibson, and have been written by experienced senior teachers and examiners in line with the new Higher for CfE syllabus and assessment outlines, Spring 2014. This is not SQA material but has been devised to provide further practice for Higher for CfE examinations in 2015 and beyond.

Hodder Gibson is grateful to the copyright holders, as credited on the final page of the Answer Section, for permission to use their material. Every effort has been made to trace the copyright holders and to obtain their permission for the use of copyright material. Hodder Gibson will be happy to receive information allowing us to rectify any error or omission in future editions.

Hachette UK's policy is to use papers that are natural, renewable and recyclable products and made from wood grown in sustainable forests. The logging and manufacturing processes are expected to conform to the environmental regulations of the country of origin.

Orders: please contact Bookpoint Ltd, 130 Park Drive, Milton Park, Abingdon, Oxon OX14 4SE. Telephone: (44) 01235 827720. Fax: (44) 01235 400454. Lines are open 9.00–5.00, Monday to Saturday, with a 24-hour message answering service. Visit our website at www.hoddereducation.co.uk. Hodder Gibson can be contacted direct on: Tel: 0141 848 1609; Fax: 0141 889 6315; email: hoddergibson@hodder.co.uk

This collection first published in 2015 by
Hodder Gibson, an imprint of Hodder Education,
An Hachette UK Company
2a Christie Street
Paisley PA1 1NB

Typeset by Aptara, Inc.

Printed in the UK

A catalogue record for this title is available from the British Library

ISBN: 978-1-4718-6069-0

3 2 1

2016 2015

Introduction

Study Skills – what you need to know to pass exams!

Pause for thought

Many students might skip quickly through a page like this. After all, we all know how to revise. Do you really though?

Think about this:

"IF YOU ALWAYS DO WHAT YOU ALWAYS DO, YOU WILL ALWAYS GET WHAT YOU HAVE ALWAYS GOT."

Do you like the grades you get? Do you want to do better? If you get full marks in your assessment, then that's great! Change nothing! This section is just to help you get that little bit better than you already are.

There are two main parts to the advice on offer here. The first part highlights fairly obvious things but which are also very important. The second part makes suggestions about revision that you might not have thought about but which WILL help you.

Part 1

DOH! It's so obvious but …

Start revising in good time

Don't leave it until the last minute – this will make you panic.

Make a revision timetable that sets out work time AND play time.

Sleep and eat!

Obvious really, and very helpful. Avoid arguments or stressful things too – even games that wind you up. You need to be fit, awake and focused!

Know your place!

Make sure you know exactly **WHEN and WHERE** your exams are.

Know your enemy!

Make sure you know what to expect in the exam.

How is the paper structured?

How much time is there for each question?

What types of question are involved?

Which topics seem to come up time and time again?

Which topics are your strongest and which are your weakest?

Are all topics compulsory or are there choices?

Learn by DOING!

There is no substitute for past papers and practice papers – they are simply essential! Tackling this collection of papers and answers is exactly the right thing to be doing as your exams approach.

Part 2

People learn in different ways. Some like low light, some bright. Some like early morning, some like evening or night. Some prefer warm, some prefer cold. But everyone uses their BRAIN and the brain works when it is active. Passive learning – sitting gazing at notes – is the most INEFFICIENT way to learn anything. Below you will find tips and ideas for making your revision more effective and maybe even more enjoyable. What follows gets your brain active, and active learning works!

Activity 1 – Stop and review

Step 1

When you have done no more than 5 minutes of revision reading STOP!

Step 2

Write a heading in your own words which sums up the topic you have been revising.

Step 3

Write a summary of what you have revised in no more than two sentences. Don't fool yourself by saying, "I know it, but I cannot put it into words". That just means you don't know it well enough. If you cannot write your summary, revise that section again, knowing that you must write a summary at the end of it. Many of you will have notebooks full of blue/black ink writing. Many of the pages will not be especially attractive or memorable so try to liven them up a bit with colour as you are reviewing and rewriting. **This is a great memory aid, and memory is the most important thing.**

Activity 2 – Use technology!

Why should everything be written down? Have you thought about "mental" maps, diagrams, cartoons and colour to help you learn? And rather than write down notes, why not record your revision material?

What about having a text message revision session with friends? Keep in touch with them to find out how and what they are revising and share ideas and questions.

Why not make a video diary where you tell the camera what you are doing, what you think you have learned and what you still have to do? No one has to see or hear it, but the process of having to organise your thoughts in a formal way to explain something is a very important learning practice.

Be sure to make use of electronic files. You could begin to summarise your class notes. Your typing might be slow, but it will get faster and the typed notes will be easier to read than the scribbles in your class notes. Try to add different fonts and colours to make your work stand out. You can easily Google relevant pictures, cartoons and diagrams which you can copy and paste to make your work more attractive and **MEMORABLE**.

Activity 3 – This is it. Do this and you will know lots!

Step 1

In this task you must be very honest with yourself! Find the SQA syllabus for your subject (www.sqa.org.uk). Look at how it is broken down into main topics called MANDATORY knowledge. That means stuff you MUST know.

Step 2

BEFORE you do ANY revision on this topic, write a list of everything that you already know about the subject. It might be quite a long list but you only need to write it once. It shows you all the information that is already in your long-term memory so you know what parts you do not need to revise!

Step 3

Pick a chapter or section from your book or revision notes. Choose a fairly large section or a whole chapter to get the most out of this activity.

With a buddy, use Skype, Facetime, Twitter or any other communication you have, to play the game "If this is the answer, what is the question?". For example, if you are revising Geography and the answer you provide is "meander", your buddy would have to make up a question like "What is the word that describes a feature of a river where it flows slowly and bends often from side to side?".

Make up 10 "answers" based on the content of the chapter or section you are using. Give this to your buddy to solve while you solve theirs.

Step 4

Construct a wordsearch of at least 10 X 10 squares. You can make it as big as you like but keep it realistic. Work together with a group of friends. Many apps allow you to make wordsearch puzzles online. The words and phrases can go in any direction and phrases can be split. Your puzzle must only contain facts linked to the topic you are revising. Your task is to find 10 bits of information to hide in your puzzle, but you must not repeat information that you used in Step 3. DO NOT show where the words are. Fill up empty squares with random letters. Remember to keep a note of where your answers are hidden but do not show your friends. When you have a completed puzzle, exchange it with a friend to solve each other's puzzle.

Step 5

Now make up 10 questions (not "answers" this time) based on the same chapter used in the previous two tasks. Again, you must find NEW information that you have not yet used. Now it's getting hard to find that new information! Again, give your questions to a friend to answer.

Step 6

As you have been doing the puzzles, your brain has been actively searching for new information. Now write a NEW LIST that contains only the new information you have discovered when doing the puzzles. Your new list is the one to look at repeatedly for short bursts over the next few days. Try to remember more and more of it without looking at it. After a few days, you should be able to add words from your second list to your first list as you increase the information in your long-term memory.

FINALLY! Be inspired...

Make a list of different revision ideas and beside each one write **THINGS I HAVE** tried, **THINGS I WILL** try and **THINGS I MIGHT** try. Don't be scared of trying something new.

And remember – "FAIL TO PREPARE AND PREPARE TO FAIL!"

Higher Human Biology

The practice papers in this book give an overall and comprehensive coverage of assessment of **Knowledge** and **Skills of Scientific Inquiry** for the new CfE Higher Human Biology.

We recommend that you refer to Higher Human Biology Course Support Notes pages 9–56 from the SQA website at www.sqa.org.uk. You should note that in your examination only the material included in the Mandatory Course key areas can be examined. Skills of Scientific Enquiry described on pages 59–62 are also examined.

The course

The Higher Human Biology Course consists of two full National Units, which are Human Cells and Physiology, and two half National Units, which are Neurobiology and Health and Communication and Immunology and Public Health. In each of the Units you will be assessed on your ability to demonstrate and apply knowledge of Human Biology and to demonstrate and apply skills of scientific inquiry. Candidates must also complete an Assignment in which they research a topic in biology and write it up as a report. They also take a Course examination.

How the course is graded

To achieve a course award for Higher Human Biology you must pass all four National Unit Assessments which will be assessed by your school or college on a pass or fail basis. The grade you get depends on the following two course assessments, which are set and graded by SQA.

1. An 800–1200 word report based on an Assignment, which is worth 17% of the grade. The Assignment is marked out of 20 marks, with 15 of the marks being for scientific inquiry skills and 5 marks for the application of knowledge.

2. A written course examination is worth the remaining 83% of the grade. The examination is marked out of 100 marks, most of which are for the demonstration and application of knowledge although there are also marks available for skills of scientific inquiry.

This book should help you practice the examination part! To pass Higher Human Biology with a C grade you will need about 50% of the 120 marks available for the Assignment and the Course Examination combined. For a B you will need roughly 60% and, for an A, roughly 70%.

The course examination

The Course Examination is a single question paper in two sections.

- **The first section** is an objective test with 20 multiple choice items for 20 marks.
- **The second section** is a mix of restricted and extended response questions worth between 1 and 9 marks each for a total of 80 marks. The majority of the marks test knowledge with an emphasis on the application of knowledge. The remainder, test the application of scientific inquiry, analysis and problem solving skills. There will be a choice offered in the longest questions.

Altogether, there are 100 marks and you will have 2 hours and 30 minutes to complete the paper. The majority of the marks will be straightforward and linked to grade C but some questions are more demanding and are linked to grade A.

General tips and hints

You should download a copy of the Course Assessment Specification (CAS) for Higher Human Biology from the SQA website. This document tells you what can be tested in your examination. It is worth spending some time on this document.

This book contains four practice Higher examination papers. One is the SQA specimen paper and there are three further model papers. Each paper has been carefully assembled to be as similar as possible to a typical Higher Human Biology Paper. Notice how similar they all are in the way in which they are laid out and the types of question they ask – your own course examination is going to be very similar as well, so the value of the papers is obvious! Each paper can be attempted in its entirety or groups of questions on a particular topic or skill area can be attempted. If you are trying a whole examination paper from this book, give yourself 2 hours and 30 minutes maximum to complete it. The questions in each paper are laid out in Unit order. Make sure that you spend time in using the answer section to mark your own work – it is especially useful if you can get someone to help you with this.

The marking instructions give acceptable answers with alternatives. You could even grade your work on an A–D basis. The following hints and tips are related to examination techniques as well as avoiding common mistakes. Remember that if you hit problems with a question, you should ask your teacher for help.

Section 1

20 multiple-choice items   20 marks

- Answer on the grid.
- Do not spend more than 30 minutes on this section.
- Some individual questions might take longer to answer than others – this is quite normal and make sure you use scrap paper if a calculation or any working is needed.
- Some questions can be answered instantly – again, this is normal.
- Do not leave blanks – complete the grid for each question as you work through.
- Try to answer each question in your head without looking at the options. If your answer is there you are home and dry!
- If you are not certain, choose the answer that seemed most attractive on first reading the answer options.
- If you are guessing, try to eliminate options before making your guess. If you can eliminate three – you are left with the correct answer even if you do not recognise it!

Section 2

Restricted and extended response   80 marks

- Spend about 2 hours on this section.
- Answer on the question paper. Try to write neatly and keep your answers on the support lines if possible – the lines are designed to take the full answer!
- A clue to answer length is the mark allocation – most questions are restricted to 1 mark and the answer can be quite short. If there are 2–4 marks available, your answer will need to be extended and may well have two, three or even four parts.
- The questions are usually laid out in Unit sequence but remember some questions are designed to cover more than one Unit.
- The C-type questions usually start with "State", "Identify", "Give" or "Name" and often need only a word or two in response. They will usually be for one mark each.
- Questions that begin with "Explain" and "Describe" are usually A types and are likely to have more than one part to the full answer. You will usually have to write a sentence or two and there may be two or even three marks available.
- Make sure you read questions over twice before trying to answer – there is often very important information within the question and you are unlikely to be short of time in this examination.

- Using abbreviations like DNA and ATP is fine and the bases of DNA can be given as A, T, G and C. The Higher Human Biology Course Assessment Support Notes will give you the acceptable abbreviations.
- Don't worry that a few questions are in unfamiliar contexts, that's the idea! Just keep calm and read the questions carefully.
- If a question contains a choice, be sure to spend a minute or two making the best choice for you.
- In experimental questions, you must be aware of what variables are, why controls are needed and how reliability and validity might be improved. It is worth spending time on these ideas – they are essential and will come up year after year.
- Some candidates like to use a highlighter pen to help them focus on the essential points of longer questions – this is a great technique.
- Remember that a conclusion can be seen from data, whereas an explanation will usually require you to supply some background knowledge as well.
- Remember to "use values from the graph" when describing graphical information in words if you are asked to do so.
- Plot graphs carefully and join the plot points using a ruler. Include zeros on your scale where appropriate and use the data table headings for the axes labels.
- Look out for graphs with two Y-axes – these need extra special concentration and anyone can make a mistake!
- If there is a space for calculation given – you will very likely need to use it! A calculator is essential.
- The main types of calculation tend to be ratios, averages, percentages and percentage change – make sure you can do these common calculations.
- Answers to calculations will not usually have more than two decimal places.
- Give units in calculation answers if they are not already given in the answer space.
- Do not leave blanks. Always have a go, using the language in the question if you can.

Good luck!

Remember that the rewards for passing Higher Human Biology are well worth it! Your pass will help you get the future you want for yourself. In the exam, be confident in your own ability. If you're not sure how to answer a question, trust your instincts and just give it a go anyway.

Keep calm and don't panic! GOOD LUCK!

National
Qualifications
SPECIMEN ONLY

SQ25/H/02

Human Biology
Section 1 — Questions

Date — Not applicable

Duration — 2 hours and 30 minutes

Instructions for the completion of Section 1 are given on *Page two* of your question and answer booklet SQ25/H/02.

Record your answers on the answer grid on *Page three* of your question and answer booklet.

Before leaving the examination room you must give your question and answer booklet to the Invigilator; if you do not you may lose all the marks for this paper.

SECTION 1 — 20 marks

Attempt ALL questions

1. The diagram below shows two chromosomes, M and N, before and after a chromosomal mutation.

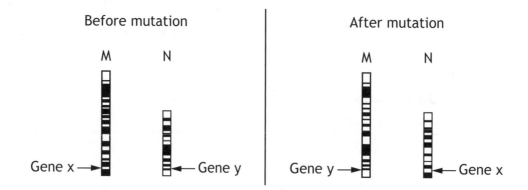

   The form of mutation that has taken place is a

   A   translocation

   B   duplication

   C   insertion

   D   deletion.

2. Amplification of DNA by PCR commences with 1000 DNA molecules in the reaction tube. How many DNA molecules would be present after four cycles of PCR?

   A   4000

   B   8000

   C   16000

   D   32000

3. Which of the following statements about slow twitch muscle fibres is correct?

   A   They cannot sustain contractions for as long as fast twitch muscle fibres.

   B   They have many more mitochondria than fast twitch muscle fibres.

   C   They are better for activities like weightlifting and sprinting than fast twitch muscle fibres.

   D   They store fuel mainly as glycogen while fast twitch muscle fibres store fuel as fat.

4. The table below contains information about four semen samples.

	Semen sample			
	A	B	C	D
Number of sperm in sample (millions/cm³)	40	30	20	60
Active sperm (%)	50	60	75	40
Abnormal sperm (%)	30	65	10	70

Which semen sample has the highest number of active sperm?

5. In which of the following situations might a fetus be at risk from Rhesus antibodies produced by the mother?

	Father	Mother
A	Rhesus positive	Rhesus negative
B	Rhesus positive	Rhesus positive
C	Rhesus negative	Rhesus negative
D	Rhesus negative	Rhesus positive

6. The family tree below shows the pattern of inheritance of a genetic condition.

Unaffected female   x   Unaffected male

Affected female

The allele responsible for this condition is both

A   sex-linked and recessive

B   sex-linked and dominant

C   autosomal and recessive

D   autosomal and dominant.

7. The graph below shows the growth, in length, of a human fetus.

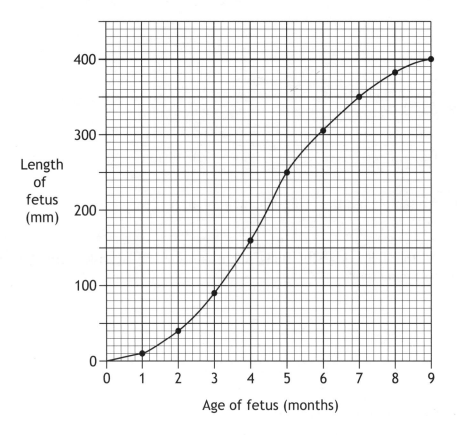

Age of fetus (months)

What is the percentage increase in length of the fetus during the final four months of pregnancy?

A   33·3%

B   60·0%

C   62·5%

D   150·0%

8. Cystic fibrosis is a genetic condition caused by an allele that is not sex-linked.

A child is born with cystic fibrosis despite neither parent having the condition.

The parents are going to have a second child.

What is the percentage chance this child will have cystic fibrosis?

A   75%

B   67%

C   50%

D   25%

9.   The duration of the stages in an individual's cardiac cycle are shown in the table below.

Stage	Duration (s)
Diastole	0·4
Atrial systole	0·1
Ventricular systole	0·3

What is the heart rate of this individual?

A   48 beats per minute

B   75 beats per minute

C   80 beats per minute

D   150 beats per minute

10.   The diagram below shows a cross-section of the heart.

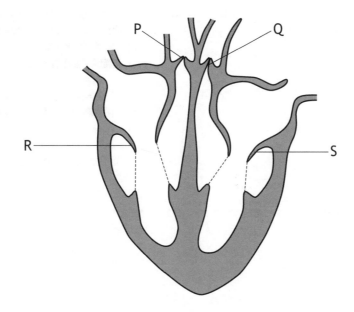

Which of the following statements describes the movement of the valves during ventricular systole?

A   Valves P and Q open and valves R and S close

B   Valves P and R open and valves Q and S close

C   Valves P and Q close and valves R and S open

D   Valves P and R close and valves Q and S open

11. Which of the following statements about lipoprotein is correct?

    A   LDL transports cholesterol from body cells to the heart

    B   LDL transports cholesterol from body cells to the liver

    C   HDL transports cholesterol from body cells to the heart

    D   HDL transports cholesterol from body cells to the liver

12. The graphs below contain information about the population of Britain.

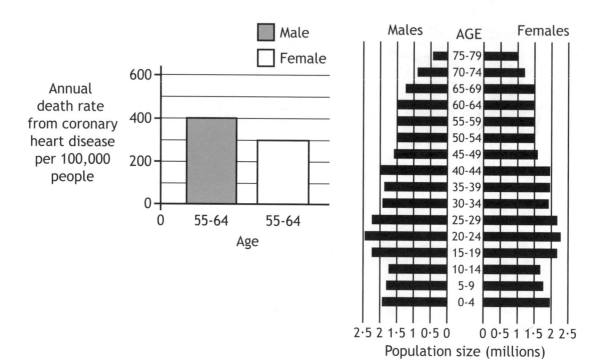

The number of British women between 55 and 64 years of age who die from coronary heart disease annually is

    A   300

    B   4500

    C   9000

    D   21000.

13. The transformation of information into a form that memory can accept is called

    A   shaping

    B   retrieval

    C   encoding

    D   storage.

14. The diagram below shows a test on a man who had a damaged corpus callosum.

This meant that he could no longer transfer information between his right and left cerebral hemispheres.

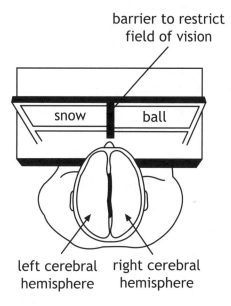

Some of the functions of each hemisphere are described in the table below.

Left cerebral hemisphere	Right cerebral hemisphere
processes information from right eye	processes information from left eye
controls language production	controls spatial task co-ordination

The man was asked to look straight ahead and then the words "snow" and "ball" were flashed briefly on the screen as shown.

What would the man say that he had just seen?

A   Snow

B   Ball

C   Snowball

D   Nothing

15. Which of the following statements about the action of recreational drugs on brain neurochemistry is correct?

A Desensitisation results from an increase in the number of neurotransmitter receptors due to the use of drugs that are agonists

B Desensitisation results from an increase in the number of neurotransmitter receptors due to the use of drugs that are antagonists

C Sensitisation results from an increase in the number of neurotransmitter receptors due to the use of drugs that are agonists

D Sensitisation results from an increase in the number of neurotransmitter receptors due to the use of drugs that are antagonists

16. An investigation was carried out to determine how long it takes students to learn to run a finger maze.

A blindfolded student was allowed to run the maze on ten occasions.

The results are given in the table below.

Trial	Time (s)
1	23
2	20
3	26
4	12
5	18
6	10
7	6
8	7
9	6
10	6

Which of the following changes to the investigation would make the results more reliable?

A Allowing other students to try to run the maze ten times.

B Allowing the same student some additional trials on the same maze.

C Changing the shape of the maze and allowing the same student to repeat ten trials.

D Recording the times to one decimal place.

17. Which of the following is not part of the inflammatory response?

A   Vasodilation

B   Release of histamine

C   Production of antibodies

D   Increased capillary permeability

18. The diagram below represents clonal selection in lymphocytes.

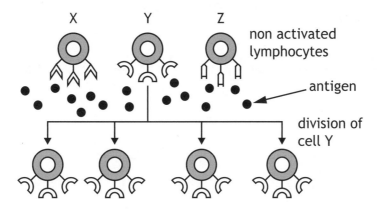

What stimulates the division of cell Y?

A   The presence of lymphocytes X and Z

B   The presence of an antigen in the blood

C   The binding of antibodies to receptors on the cell membrane

D   The binding of antigens to receptors on the cell membrane

19. Two groups of subjects were used when carrying out clinical trials of a vaccine.
     One group was given the vaccine while the other group was given a placebo.
     The purpose of the placebo was to

A   reduce experimental error

B   ensure a valid comparison can be made

C   allow a statistical analysis of the results to be made

D   ensure that researchers are unaware who has been vaccinated.

20. The table below contains data about a worldwide infection in 2009.

	Number of adults	Number of children
Had this infection at the start of 2009	$30 \cdot 8 \times 10^6$	$2 \cdot 5 \times 10^6$
Contracted this infection during 2009	$2 \cdot 2 \times 10^6$	$0 \cdot 4 \times 10^6$
Died from this infection during 2009	$1 \cdot 6 \times 10^6$	$0 \cdot 2 \times 10^6$

How many people in the world had this infection at the start of 2010?

A $35 \cdot 9 \times 10^6$

B $34 \cdot 1 \times 10^6$

C $33 \cdot 3 \times 10^6$

D $31 \cdot 5 \times 10^6$

[END OF SECTION 1. NOW ATTEMPT THE QUESTIONS IN SECTION 2
OF YOUR QUESTION AND ANSWER BOOKLET.]

National Qualifications
SPECIMEN ONLY

Mark

SQ25/H/01

Human Biology
Section 1 — Answer Grid and Section 2

Date — Not applicable

Duration — 2 hours and 30 minutes

Fill in these boxes and read what is printed below.

Full name of centre

Town

Forename(s)

Surname

Number of seat

Date of birth

Day	Month	Year
D D	M M	Y Y

Scottish candidate number

Total marks — 100

SECTION 1 — 20 marks

Attempt ALL questions.

Instructions for completion of Section 1 are given on *Page two*.

SECTION 2 — 80 marks

Attempt ALL questions.

Write your answers in the spaces provided. Additional space for answers and rough work is provided at the end of this booklet. If you use this space, write clearly the number of the question you are attempting. Any rough work must be written in this booklet. You should score through your rough work when you have written your fair copy.

Use **blue** or **black** ink.

Before leaving the examination room you must give this booklet to the Invigilator; if you do not, you may lose all the marks for this paper.

SECTION 1— 20 marks

The questions for Section 1 are contained in the question paper SQ25/H/02.
Read these and record your answers on the answer grid on *Page three* opposite.
Do NOT use gel pens.

1. The answer to each question is **either** A, B, C or D. Decide what your answer is, then fill in the appropriate bubble (see sample question below).

2. There is **only one correct** answer to each question.

3. Any rough working should be done on the additional space for answers and rough work at the end of this booklet.

Sample Question

The digestive enzyme pepsin is most active in the

   A   mouth

   B   stomach

   C   duodenum

   D   pancreas.

The correct answer is **B**—stomach. The answer **B** bubble has been clearly filled in (see below).

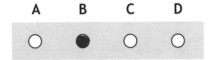

Changing an answer

If you decide to change your answer, cancel your first answer by putting a cross through it (see below) and fill in the answer you want. The answer below has been changed to **D**.

If you then decide to change back to an answer you have already scored out, put a tick (✓) to the **right** of the answer you want, as shown below:

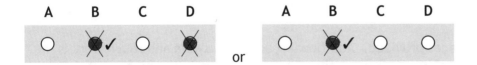

SECTION 1 — Answer Grid

	A	B	C	D
1	○	○	○	○
2	○	○	○	○
3	○	○	○	○
4	○	○	○	○
5	○	○	○	○
6	○	○	○	○
7	○	○	○	○
8	○	○	○	○
9	○	○	○	○
10	○	○	○	○
11	○	○	○	○
12	○	○	○	○
13	○	○	○	○
14	○	○	○	○
15	○	○	○	○
16	○	○	○	○
17	○	○	○	○
18	○	○	○	○
19	○	○	○	○
20	○	○	○	○

MARKS | DO NOT WRITE IN THIS MARGIN

SECTION 2 — 80 marks

Attempt ALL questions

Note that question 14 contains a choice.

1. The human body contains many specialised cells, all of which have developed from stem cells in the early embryo.

Nerve cells

Liver cells

Cardiac muscle cells

(a) Name the process by which a stem cell develops into a specialised body cell and explain how this process occurs.　　2

Process _____

Explanation _____

_____

(b) Both germline and somatic cells retain the ability to divide.

　(i) State the type of cell division that only occurs in germline cells.　　1

　　_____

　(ii) Explain why mutations in germline cells are potentially more serious than mutations in somatic cells.　　1

　　_____

　　_____

(c) A company has developed a drug that could be used to treat the symptoms of an inherited disease. Before proceeding to clinical trials using volunteers, the company decides to carry out additional tests in the laboratory using stem cells.

　Describe one ethical consideration that might have influenced this decision to use stem cells.　　1

　_____

　_____

MARKS | DO NOT WRITE IN THIS MARGIN

2. The diagram below shows stages in the synthesis of a polypeptide.

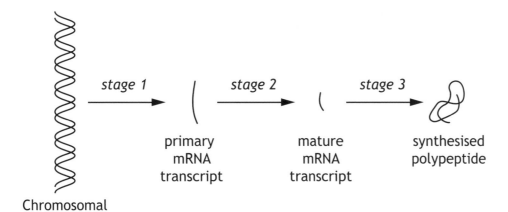

stage 1 → primary mRNA transcript   stage 2 → mature mRNA transcript   stage 3 → synthesised polypeptide

Chromosomal DNA

(a) Name the enzyme that catalyses stage 1 of this process.   1

_____

(b) Name stage 3 and state the exact location where it occurs within a cell.   1

Name _____

Location _____

(c) (i) Explain why the primary mRNA transcript is so much shorter than chromosomal DNA.   1

_____

_____

(ii) Explain why the mature mRNA transcript is shorter than the primary mRNA transcript.   1

_____

_____

MARKS | DO NOT WRITE IN THIS MARGIN

3. An experiment was carried out to investigate the effect of substrate concentration on the production of an end-product in an enzyme controlled reaction.

The enzyme urease was used which breaks down urea into ammonia.

$$\text{urea} \xrightarrow{\text{urease}} \text{ammonia}$$

Urease and urea solutions were mixed together and added to test tubes containing agar jelly as shown in the diagram below.

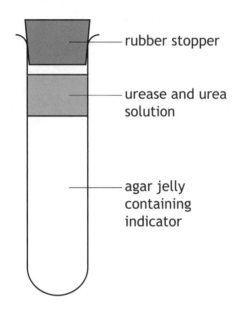

— rubber stopper

— urease and urea solution

— agar jelly containing indicator

Five different concentrations of urea solution were added.

During the reaction the ammonia produced diffused through the agar jelly changing the indicator from yellow to blue.

The length of the agar jelly stained blue was measured after the experiment had been allowed to run for 48 hours.

The results of the experiment are shown in the table below.

Urea concentration added (molar)	Average length of agar jelly stained blue (mm)
0·03	2
0·06	4
0·13	8
0·25	16
0·50	32

MARKS | DO NOT WRITE IN THIS MARGIN

3.　(continued)

(a)　Plot a line graph to illustrate the results of the experiment.

(Additional graph paper, if required, can be found on *Page twenty-six*)　2

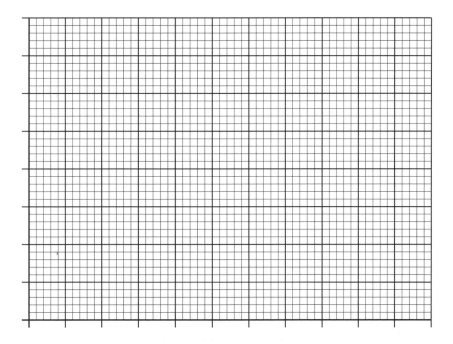

(b)　(i)　Name **one** variable that should be controlled when setting up this experiment.　1

_____

(ii)　Name **one** variable that should be kept constant during the 48 hours of this experiment.　1

_____

(c)　Give the feature of this experiment that makes the results reliable.　1

_____

_____

(d)　Explain why the test tubes were left for 48 hours before the results were obtained.　1

_____

_____

MARKS | DO NOT WRITE IN THIS MARGIN

3. **(continued)**

(e) State **one** conclusion that can be drawn from the results of this experiment.

1

_____

_____

(f) Using the **information in the table**, predict the length of agar jelly that would have been stained blue if a 0·75 molar urea solution had been used in the experiment.

1

Space for calculation

_____ mm

(g) Thiourea is a competitive inhibitor of urease.

In another experiment, a test tube of agar jelly was set up containing the urease solution, 0·5 molar urea solution and thiourea.

After 48 hours only 7mm of agar jelly had turned blue.

(i) Explain why less agar jelly turned blue in this experiment than in the first experiment, which also used a 0·5 molar urea solution.

1

_____

_____

(ii) Suggest why 7mm of agar jelly turned blue in this experiment.

1

_____

_____

MARKS | DO NOT WRITE IN THIS MARGIN

4. The diagram below represents the glycolysis stage of respiration in a muscle cell.

           Phase 1   *Phase 2*

    glucose   ⟶   intermediate   ⟶   pyruvate
    compounds

    (a) Phase 1 is the energy investment stage of glycolysis while phase 2 is the energy pay-off stage of glycolysis.

    Describe what happens during the energy investment and energy pay-off phases of glycolysis.　　**2**

    Energy investment phase _____

    _____

    Energy pay-off phase _____

    _____

    (b) Once pyruvate has been formed it can be converted into two different compounds, depending on the conditions.

    Name one of these compounds and state under what conditions it would be produced.　　**2**

    _____

    _____

    (c) Many athletes take creatine supplements to improve their sporting performance.

    State whether sprinters or marathon runners would gain the greatest benefit from taking creatine and give a reason for your choice.　　**1**

    Athlete _____

    Reason _____

    _____

MARKS | DO NOT WRITE IN THIS MARGIN

5.   Sickle cell disease is an autosomal blood disorder in which a faulty form of haemoglobin, called haemoglobin S, is produced. This protein is an inefficient carrier of oxygen.

The allele for normal haemoglobin (H) is incompletely dominant to the allele for haemoglobin S (S).

Heterozygous individuals (HS) suffer from a milder condition called sickle cell trait.

The pedigree chart below shows the incidence of these conditions in three generations of a family.

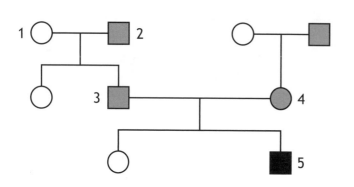

☐ male with sickle cell trait

■ male with sickle cell disease

○ unaffected female

● female with sickle cell trait

(a)   State the genotype of individual 5.   1

_____

(b)   Individuals 3 and 4 go on to have a 3rd child.

State the percentage chance that this child will have the same genotype as the parents.   1

Space for calculation

_____ %

(c)   Sickle cell disease is caused by a substitution mutation in the gene that codes for haemoglobin.

(i)   Describe how this form of mutation affects the structure of the gene.   1

_____

_____

(ii)   Explain how this might change the structure of a protein such as haemoglobin.   1

_____

_____

MARKS | DO NOT WRITE IN THIS MARGIN

5. (continued)

(d) During IVF treatment, it is possible to detect single gene disorders in fertilised eggs before they are implanted into the mother.

Give the term that describes this procedure.   **1**

_____

(e) It has been discovered that the gene that codes for fetal haemoglobin is unaffected by the substitution mutation that causes sickle cell disease.

This gene is "switched off" at birth.

Use this information to suggest how a drug designed to treat sickle cell disease in young children could function.   **1**

_____

_____

_____

MARKS | DO NOT WRITE IN THIS MARGIN

6. The diagram below represents a section through an artery.

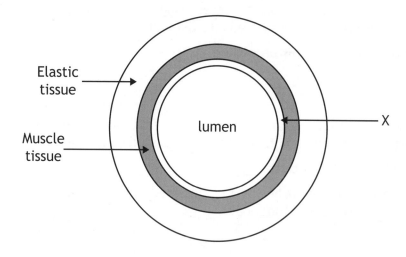

Elastic tissue

Muscle tissue

lumen

X

(a) Describe how the presence of muscle tissue in the artery wall helps to control the flow of blood around the body.

1

(b) Describe how an atheroma forming under layer X may lead to the formation of a blood clot and state the possible effects of this.

5

Space for answer

7. The graph below shows how an individual's heart rate and stroke volume changed as their oxygen uptake increased during exercise.

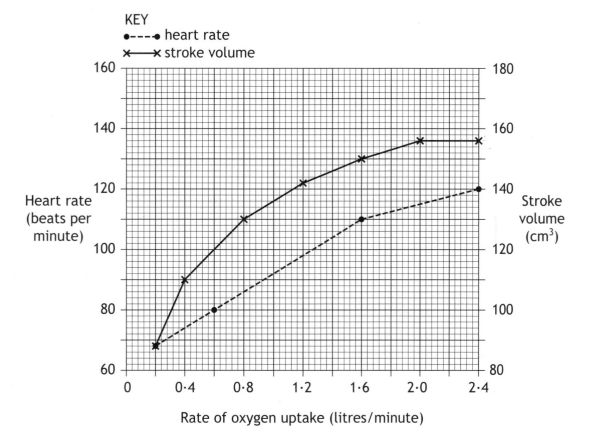

(a) (i) State the individual's heart rate when the rate of oxygen uptake was 1·2 litres/minute. **1**

_____

(ii) Using data from the graph, describe how the stroke volume changed as oxygen uptake increased. **1**

_____

_____

(iii) State the stroke volume when the heart rate was 110 beats per minute. **1**

_____ cm³

MARKS | DO NOT WRITE IN THIS MARGIN

7. (continued)

(b) Calculate the cardiac output when the rate of oxygen uptake was 2·4 litres per minute.

Space for calculation

1

_____ litres/min

(c)   (i)   When the individual's blood pressure was measured an hour after exercise, a reading of 140/90 mm/Hg was recorded.

Explain why two figures are given for a blood pressure reading.

1

_____

_____

(ii)   The individual was diagnosed as having high blood pressure.

One of the effects of this was that their ankles regularly swelled up due to a build-up of tissue fluid.

Explain the link between high blood pressure and the build-up of tissue fluid.

2

_____

_____

_____

_____

8. The graph below shows changes in blood glucose concentration in a diabetic and a non-diabetic individual after each had consumed a glucose drink.

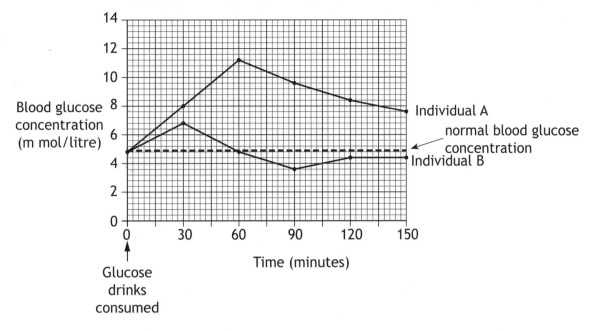

(a) (i) Choose **one** individual, A or B and indicate whether the individual is diabetic or non-diabetic.

Individual _____

Diabetic ☐   Non-diabetic ☐

Using evidence from the graph, justify your choice.   **1**

_____

_____

(ii) Using data from the graph, describe the changes that occurred in the blood glucose concentration of individual A after consuming the glucose drink.   **2**

_____

_____

_____

_____

MARKS | DO NOT WRITE IN THIS MARGIN

8.   (continued)

(b) Describe the role of insulin in the development of type 1 and type 2 diabetes.   2

Type 1 _____

_____

Type 2 _____

_____

9. The graph below shows obesity data for a European country in 2003 and 2012.

Individuals are described as obese if they have a body mass index (BMI) of 30 or greater.

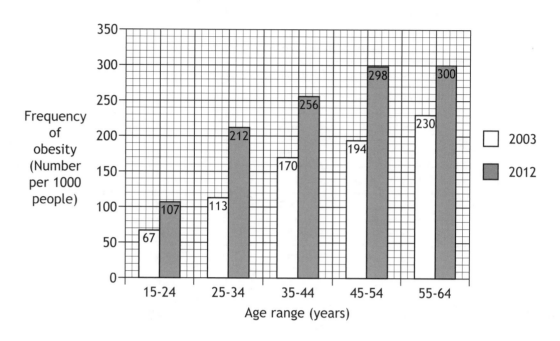

(a) (i) Describe **two** general trends shown in the graph.   2

1 _____

_____

2 _____

_____

(ii) In 2012 the number of people in this country aged 35 to 44 was 6 million.

Calculate how many people aged 35 to 44 were obese.   1

Space for calculation

Number of people _____

(b) State one piece of advice that an obese individual would be given to adapt their diet or lifestyle in order to avoid long-term health problems.   1

_____

MARKS | DO NOT WRITE IN THIS MARGIN

10. A student carried out an investigation into the effect of age on learning ability.

Eight children from three different age groups were each given five attempts to complete a twenty-piece jigsaw puzzle.

The fastest times that they achieved are shown in the table below.

	Fastest time achieved (seconds)		
	8-year-olds	12-year-olds	16-year-olds
	123	97	99
	98	68	74
	111	75	62
	138	112	67
	87	93	84
	136	83	101
	79	75	58
	120	81	55
average	111·5		75·0

(a) Calculate the average fastest time achieved by the 12 year-old children and write your answer in the table above.   **1**

Space for calculation

(b) Describe **two** additional variables that would have to be kept constant to ensure a valid comparison could be made between the three groups of children.   **2**

Variable 1 _____

_____

Variable 2 _____

_____

MARKS | DO NOT WRITE IN THIS MARGIN

10. **(continued)**

(c) State a conclusion that can be drawn from the results of this investigation.

1

_____

_____

(d) (i) Explain why the first attempt to complete the puzzle was always slower than the fifth attempt, no matter the age of the child.

1

_____

_____

(ii) Suggest why some children did not produce their fastest time on their fifth attempt.

1

_____

_____

(e) Suggest how the student could adapt the investigation to demonstrate social facilitation.

1

_____

_____

MARKS | DO NOT WRITE IN THIS MARGIN

11. The graph below shows the number of whooping cough cases over a 65 year period in a country.

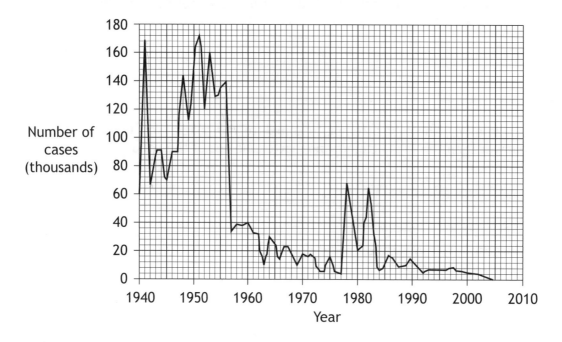

(a) (i) Using information from the graph, state the year in which a vaccine for whooping cough was introduced.   1

Year _____

(ii) Suggest a reason for the unexpected increase in the number of cases of whooping cough in 1977.   1

_____

_____

(b) The number of cases of whooping cough decreases to a very low level after 2000 because of herd immunity.

Explain what is meant by the term "herd immunity".   2

_____

_____

_____

_____

MARKS | DO NOT WRITE IN THIS MARGIN

12.   The diagrams below contain information about the causes of death and survival rates in two countries in 2010.

Figure 1 - Causes of death in countries A and B during 2010

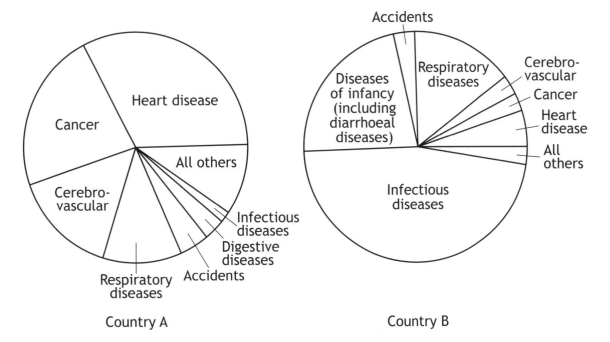

Country A

Country B

Figure 2 - Percentage survival rates in countries A and B in 2010

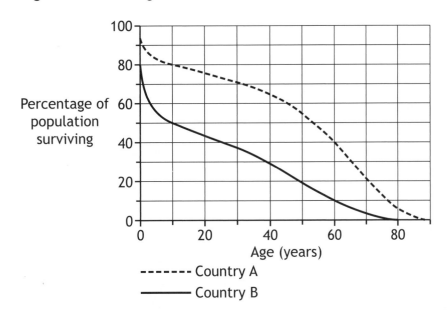

------- Country A

———— Country B

(a)   (i)   Use information from **Figure 2** to explain the lower incidence of heart disease in Country B.   1

_____

_____

MARKS | DO NOT WRITE IN THIS MARGIN

12. **(a)** **(continued)**

(ii) Give an example of how diseases of infancy can be reduced in Country B through community responsibility, other than by vaccination programmes.

1

_____

_____

(b) (i) Calculate the percentage of the population of Country A that die before the age of 10.

1

Space for calculation

_____ %

(ii) In 1950 three million babies were born in Country B.

Calculate how many of these individuals were still alive in 2010, assuming no migration occurred.

1

Space for calculation

_____

MARKS | DO NOT WRITE IN THIS MARGIN

13. Pulmonary tuberculosis (TB) is an infectious disease of the lungs caused by a bacterium.

This bacterium can also damage other organs in the body. When this happens it is called non-pulmonary TB.

The table below shows the number of reported cases of pulmonary and non-pulmonary TB in Scotland between 1981 and 2006.

Year	Number of cases of pulmonary TB	Number of cases of non-pulmonary TB
1981	659	140
1986	500	178
1991	452	97
1996	408	102
2001	275	125
2006	255	153

(a) Suggest how pulmonary TB is transmitted between individuals.   1

_____

_____

(b) (i) In which 5 year period was the greatest decrease in the total number of cases of TB?   1

Space for calculation

_____

(ii) Suggest a reason for this decrease.   1

_____

_____

(iii) Compare the trend in the number of cases of pulmonary TB with that of non-pulmonary TB between 1991 and 2006.   1

_____

_____

MARKS | DO NOT WRITE IN THIS MARGIN

13. **(b)** **(continued)**

(iv) Calculate, as a simple whole number ratio, the number of cases of pulmonary TB compared to non-pulmonary TB in 2001.   **1**

Space for calculation

_____ : _____
pulmonary TB   non-pulmonary TB

(c) Non-pulmonary TB is often associated with HIV infection.

Suggest a reason for this association.   **1**

_____

_____

MARKS | DO NOT WRITE IN THIS MARGIN

14. Answer **either** A **or** B in the space below.

A   Describe the structure and function of the autonomic nervous system.   **7**

OR

B   Describe the function and mechanism of neurotransmitter action at the synapse.   **7**

[END OF SPECIMEN QUESTION PAPER]

ADDITIONAL SPACE FOR ANSWERS AND ROUGH WORK

Additional Graph for Question 3 (a)

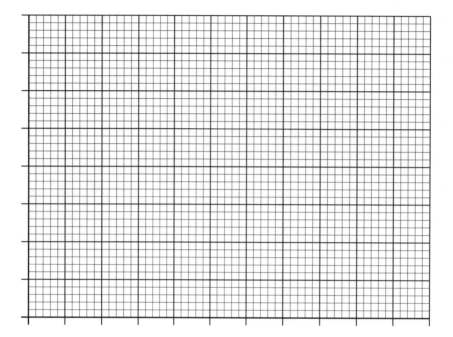

MARKS | DO NOT WRITE IN THIS MARGIN

ADDITIONAL SPACE FOR ANSWERS AND ROUGH WORK

ADDITIONAL SPACE FOR ANSWERS AND ROUGH WORK

Model Paper 1

Whilst this Model Paper has been specially commissioned by Hodder Gibson for use as practice for the Higher (for Curriculum for Excellence) exams, the key reference documents remain the SQA Specimen Paper 2014 and SQA Past Paper 2015.

HODDER
GIBSON
LEARN MORE

National
Qualifications
MODEL PAPER 1

Human Biology
Section 1—Questions

Duration — 2 hours and 30 minutes

Instructions for the completion of Section 1 are given on *Page two* of your question and answer booklet.

Record your answers on the answer grid on *Page three* of your question and answer booklet.

Before leaving the examination room you must give your question and answer booklet to the Invigilator; if you do not, you may lose all the marks for this paper.

HODDER
GIBSON
LEARN MORE

SECTION 1 — 20 marks

Attempt ALL questions

1. Which of the following diagrams shows correctly some aspects of the structure of DNA?

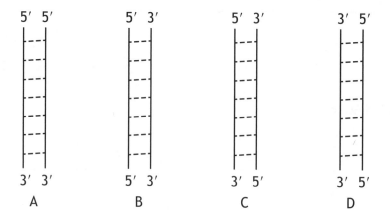

2. If 10% of the bases in a molecule of DNA are adenine, what is the ratio of adenine to guanine in the same molecule?

A   1 : 1

B   1 : 2

C   1 : 3

D   1 : 4

3. A parent DNA molecule replicates before meiosis. A cell containing a parent DNA molecule went through two rounds of cell division as shown in the diagram below.

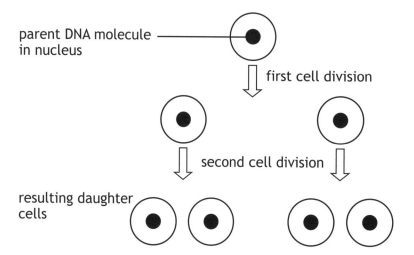

How many of the copies of the parent DNA molecule found in the resulting daughter cells would contain an original strand from the parent molecule?

A   1

B   2

C   4

D   8

4. The diagram below represents a stage in protein synthesis in a cell.

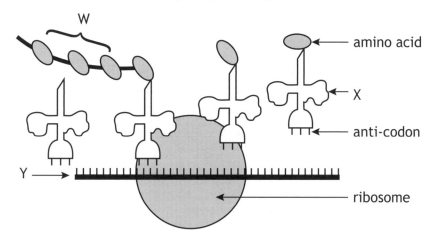

Which line in the table below identifies correctly molecules W, X and Y?

	Molecules		
	W	X	Y
A	polypeptide	tRNA	mRNA
B	tRNA	mRNA	polypeptide
C	mRNA	tRNA	polypeptide
D	polypeptide	mRNA	tRNA

5. The graph below shows the temperature changes involved in one thermal cycle of the polymerase chain reaction (PCR).

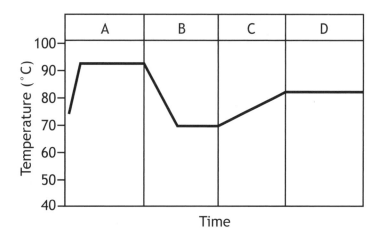

Which letter indicates when primers would bind to target sequences of DNA?

6. The graph below shows the effect of substrate concentration on the rate of an enzyme-catalysed reaction.

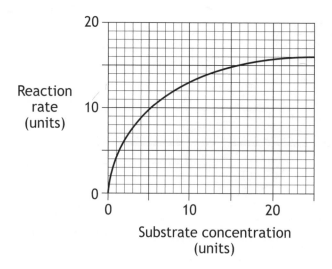

At which substrate concentration is the reaction rate equal to 75% of the maximum rate?

A   5 units

B   8 units

C   12 units

D   15 units

7. Metabolic pathways can be controlled by feedback inhibition in which

A   an end product of a pathway binds to an enzyme involved earlier in the pathway

B   an end product of a pathway binds to an enzyme involved in another pathway

C   the final substrate in a pathway binds to an enzyme involved earlier in the pathway

D   the final substrate in a pathway binds to an enzyme involved in another pathway.

8. The diagram below shows a section through seminiferous tubules in the testes.

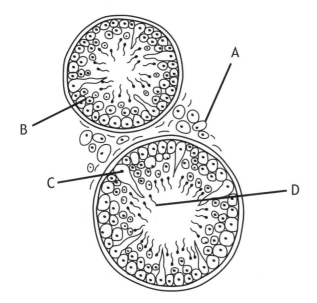

Which letter indicates a cell that produces testosterone?

9. Average sperm counts made from semen samples of groups of men from 1940 through to 2000 are shown on the graph below.

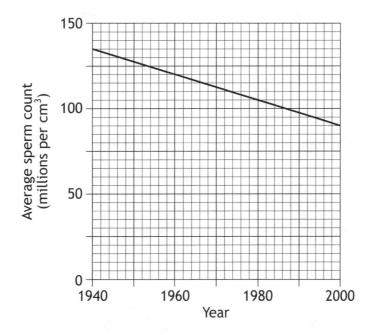

What is the average reduction in average sperm count per year?

A   0.67 million per cm^3

B   0.75 million per cm^3

C   0.92 million per cm^3

D   45 million per cm^3

10. Phenylketonuria (PKU) is a condition that affects metabolism. PKU is caused by failure to produce enzyme X shown in the metabolic pathway below.

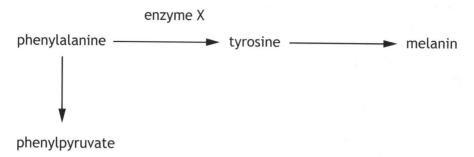

Which line in the table shows correctly the differences in concentrations of the substances in the body of an individual affected by PKU compared with the body of an unaffected individual?

	Increased concentration	Decreased concentration
A	Phenylalanine only	Tyrosine only
B	Tyrosine only	Phenylalanine only
C	Tyrosine and melanin	Phenylalanine and phenylpyruvate
D	Phenylalanine and phenylpyruvate	Tyrosine and melanin

11. Which of the diagrams below best represents correctly a cross-section through a vein?

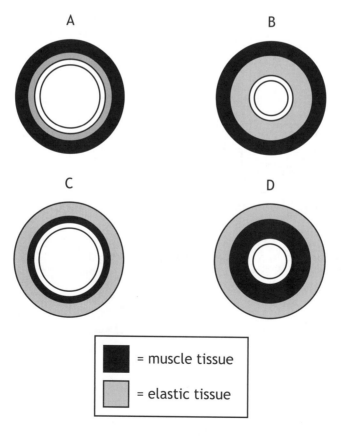

12. The diagram below shows the relationship between blood capillaries, body cells and lymph capillaries.

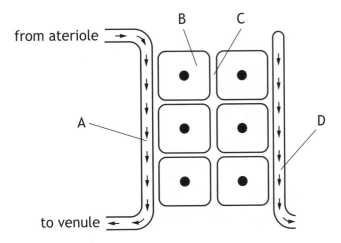

Which letter indicates the position of tissue fluid?

13. Mean arterial pressure (MAP) is a measure of blood pressure in arteries.

Pulse pressure is the difference between systolic and diastolic blood pressure.

MAP is calculated using the formula below.

   MAP = diastolic pressure + (pulse pressure/3)

The MAP of an individual with a blood pressure reading of 122/80 mmHg is

A   42 mmHg

B   56 mmHg

C   94 mmHg

D   136 mmHg.

14. Which line in the table below identifies correctly actions in the autonomic nervous system?

	Sympathetic	Parasympathetic
A	decreased secretion of saliva	increased secretion of saliva
B	increased release of gastric juice	decreased release of gastric juice
C	increased peristalsis	decreased peristalsis
D	decreased breathing rate	increased breathing rate

15. Perpetual set influences how an individual perceives an image. Some individuals perceive the image below as that of a young woman looking away and others as an old woman looking left.

Which of the following is **not** likely to play a part in perpetual set of the individuals in this case?

A   previous experience

B   binocular disparity

C   context

D   expectation

16. A young child is scratched by a cat. After this experience she shows fear of all cats.
This type of behaviour is called

A   shaping

B   internalisation

C   discrimination

D   generalisation.

17. The diagram below shows features of the relationship between short and long-term memory.

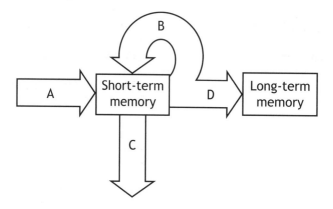

Which arrow could represent the process of displacement?

Page eight

18. The graph below shows the number of reported cases of meningitis and the number of deaths due to meningitis in the UK in 1998 to 2001.

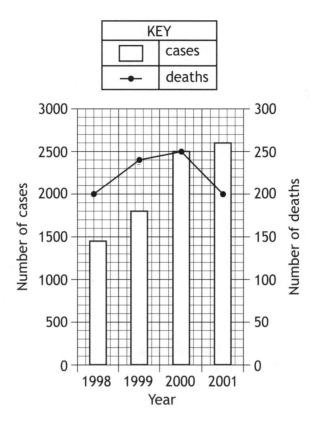

In which year was the number of deaths from meningitis less than 10% of the total number of cases in that year?

A   1998

B   1999

C   2000

D   2001

19. Adjuvants are often added to vaccines to

A   make the vaccines safer

B   enhance the immune response the vaccines trigger

C   make the immunity the vaccines produce last longer

D   ensure total removal of pathogens from the vaccines.

20. The graphs below show the effects of two injections of an antigen on the concentrations of antibody in the blood.

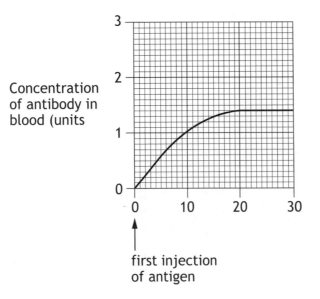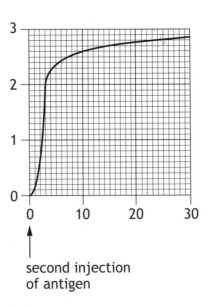

Concentration of antibody in blood (units

first injection of antigen

second injection of antigen

Time in days

By what percentage did the concentration of antibody increase 25 days after the second injection compared with 25 days after the first?

A   1%

B   25%

C   50%

D   100%

**[END OF SECTION 1. NOW ATTEMPT THE QUESTIONS IN SECTION 2
OF YOUR QUESTION AND ANSWER BOOKLET]**

National Qualifications MODEL PAPER 1

Human Biology
Section 1 — Answer Grid and Section 2

Duration — 2 hours and 30 minutes

Fill in these boxes and read what is printed below.

Full name of centre

Town

Forename(s)

Surname

Number of seat

Date of birth

Day	Month	Year
D D	M M	Y Y

Scottish candidate number

Total marks — 100

SECTION 1 — 20 marks

Attempt ALL questions.

Instructions for completion of Section 1 are given on *Page two*.

SECTION 2 — 80 marks

Attempt ALL questions.

Write your answers in the spaces provided. Additional space for answers and rough work is provided at the end of this booklet. If you use this space, write clearly the number of the question you are attempting. Any rough work must be written in this booklet. You should score through your rough work when you have written your fair copy.

Use **blue** or **black** ink.

Before leaving the examination room you must give this booklet to the Invigilator; if you do not, you may lose all the marks for this paper.

SECTION 1— 20 marks

The questions for Section 1 are contained on *Page 49*.
Read these and record your answers on the answer grid on *Page three* opposite.
Do NOT use gel pens.

1. The answer to each question is **either** A, B, C or D. Decide what your answer is, then fill in the appropriate bubble (see sample question below).

2. There is **only one correct** answer to each question.

3. Any rough working should be done on the additional space for answers and rough work at the end of this booklet.

Sample Question

The digestive enzyme pepsin is most active in the

    A   mouth

    B   stomach

    C   duodenum

    D   pancreas.

The correct answer is **B**—stomach. The answer **B** bubble has been clearly filled in (see below).

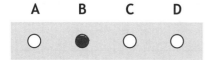

Changing an answer

If you decide to change your answer, cancel your first answer by putting a cross through it (see below) and fill in the answer you want. The answer below has been changed to **D**.

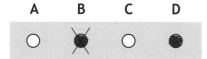

If you then decide to change back to an answer you have already scored out, put a tick (✓) to the **right** of the answer you want, as shown below:

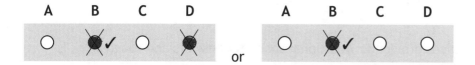

    or

SECTION 1 — Answer Grid

	A	B	C	D
1	○	○	○	○
2	○	○	○	○
3	○	○	○	○
4	○	○	○	○
5	○	○	○	○
6	○	○	○	○
7	○	○	○	○
8	○	○	○	○
9	○	○	○	○
10	○	○	○	○
11	○	○	○	○
12	○	○	○	○
13	○	○	○	○
14	○	○	○	○
15	○	○	○	○
16	○	○	○	○
17	○	○	○	○
18	○	○	○	○
19	○	○	○	○
20	○	○	○	○

MARKS | DO NOT WRITE IN THIS MARGIN

SECTION 2 — 80 marks

Attempt ALL questions

(Note that question 15 contains a choice)

1. The diagram below shows the role of embryonic stem cells in the development of a human embryo.

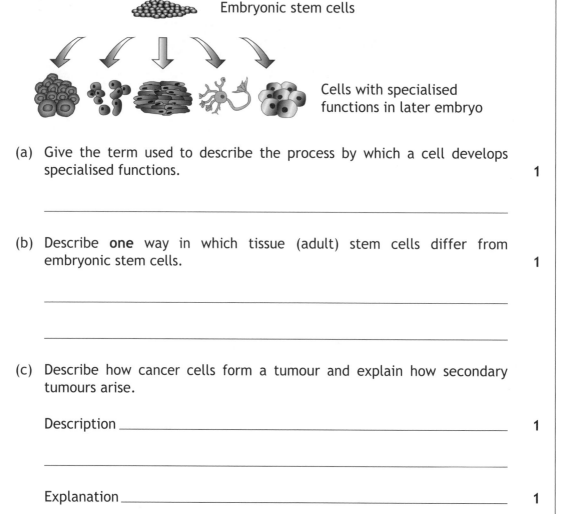

Early human embryo

Embryonic stem cells

Cells with specialised functions in later embryo

(a) Give the term used to describe the process by which a cell develops specialised functions.

1

_____

(b) Describe **one** way in which tissue (adult) stem cells differ from embryonic stem cells.

1

_____

_____

(c) Describe how cancer cells form a tumour and explain how secondary tumours arise.

Description _____

1

_____

Explanation _____

1

_____

MARKS | DO NOT WRITE IN THIS MARGIN

2. The diagram below shows part of a DNA template strand and a part of a primary RNA transcript synthesised from it.

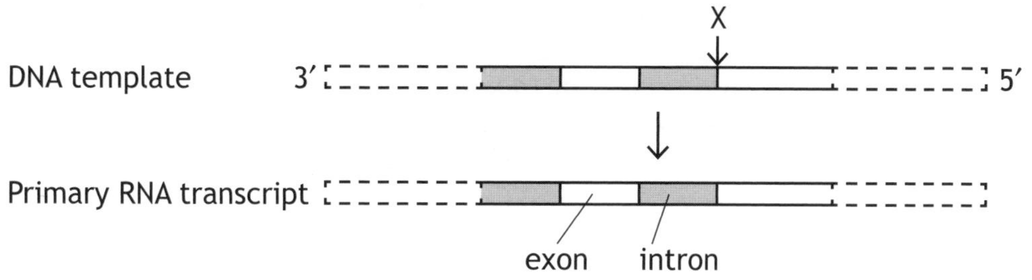

X

DNA template   3' [- - - - - - -]■■■[   ]■■■[   ][- - - - - - -] 5'

↓

Primary RNA transcript [- - - - - - -]■■■[ ]■■■[   ][- - - - - - -]

exon   intron

(a) Give the term used to describe the process shown in the diagram.   **1**

_____

(b) DNA is encoded in triplet sequences.

Explain what is meant by this.   **1**

_____

_____

(c) Using information in the diagram:

(i) Explain what is meant by the term antiparallel.   **1**

_____

_____

(ii) Describe a possible effect on the primary RNA transcript of a single nucleotide mutation at point X on the DNA template.   **1**

_____

_____

MARKS | DO NOT WRITE IN THIS MARGIN

3. (a) The table below shows single nucleotide substitution mutations of human genes and the possible effect they may have.

Complete the table by adding correct information to the empty boxes.   **2**

Name of single nucleotide substitution	Possible effect of the mutation on the protein synthesised
	A correct amino acid replaced by an incorrect one in a polypeptide chain
Nonsense	

(b) One form of Down Syndrome is caused by a translocation chromosome mutation which produces substantial changes to an affected individual's genetic material.

(i) Describe what is meant by translocation.   **1**

_____

_____

(ii) Apart from translocation, name **one** other type chromosome mutation which can affect the structure of human chromosomes.   **1**

_____

MARKS | DO NOT WRITE IN THIS MARGIN

4. The diagram below shows some molecules involved in an enzyme-catalysed reaction in the presence of an inhibitor.

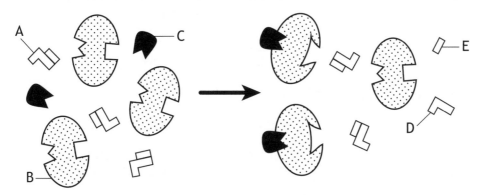

(a) Using **all** the letters from the diagram, complete the table below.   2

Molecules involved in reaction	Letter(s)
Enzyme	
Substrate	
Products	
Inhibitor	

(b) Identify the type of inhibition occurring in this example and explain how the inhibitor molecules produce their effect.

Type of inhibition _____   1

Explanation of effect _____   2

_____

_____

MARKS | DO NOT WRITE IN THIS MARGIN

5. During strenuous exercise, the following processes occur in muscle cells.

- Creatine phosphate is broken down to release energy and phosphate that are used to produce ATP as shown on the diagram below.

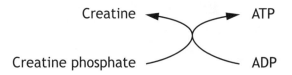

Creatine ⟶ ATP

Creatine phosphate ⟶ ADP

- Pyruvate is converted to lactic acid when oxygen becomes deficient.

The graph below shows the concentrations of creatine phosphate and lactic acid in the muscle cells of a middle distance runner over a 20 second period on a treadmill during which he jogged gently for the first 10 seconds then sprinted strenuously for 10 seconds.

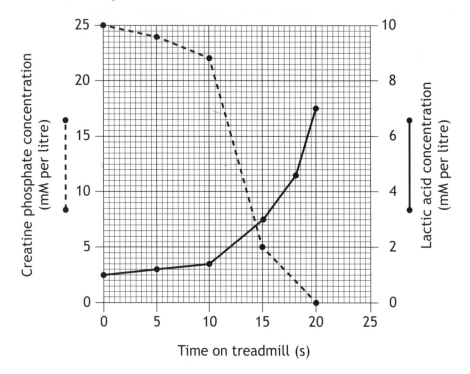

(a) (i) Give the lactic acid concentration in muscle cells after 15 seconds. **1**

_____ mM per litre

(ii) Calculate the average increase in lactic acid concentration per second over the total 20 seconds. **1**

Space for calculation

_____ mM per litre

MARKS | DO NOT WRITE IN THIS MARGIN

5. (a) (continued)

(iii) Give the creatine phosphate concentration when the lactic acid concentration was 5mM per litre.

1

Space for calculation

_____ mM per litre

(iv) Explain the reasons for the changes in concentration of the two substances shown in the graph.

Creatine phosphate _____

1

_____

Lactic acid _____

1

_____

(b) The chart below shows the percentages of fast and slow twitch muscle fibres in the muscles of the middle distance runner compared with those of athletes in other categories and in untrained individuals.

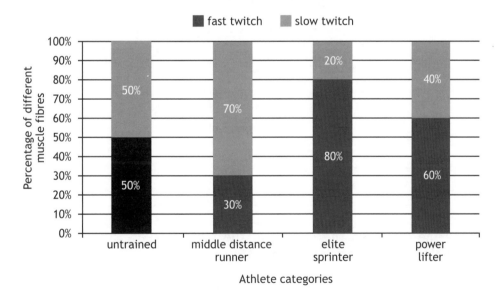

(i) Describe the differences in the percentages of muscle types in the middle distance runner compared with:

1 an untrained individual _____

1

_____

2 an elite sprinter _____

1

_____

MARKS | DO NOT WRITE IN THIS MARGIN

5. (b) (continued)

(ii) Explain how the percentages of the different fibres found in the muscles of power lifters are suitable for their activity.

1

_____

_____

6. The graph below shows the relative concentrations of three hormones in the blood plasma of a woman during a 28-day menstrual cycle.

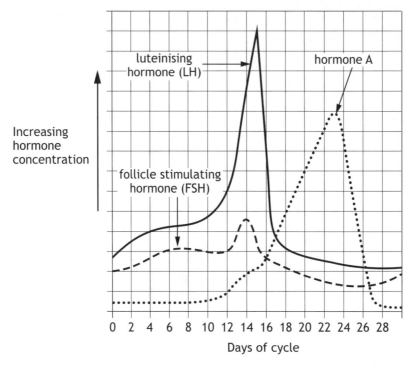

(a) Name hormone A.

1

_____

(b) Describe the effect on the ovaries of the rapid increase in lutenising hormone (LH) concentration up to day 15.

1

_____

(c) Identify the time interval during which the endometrium would be expected to reach its maximum thickness.

1

Tick (✓) the correct box

    0 – 4 days   6 – 10 days   12 – 16 days   22 –26 days

☐   ☐   ☐   ☐

MARKS | DO NOT WRITE IN THIS MARGIN

6. (continued)

(d) Predict how the levels of follicle stimulating hormone (FSH) present in the woman's blood would be different from those shown, if a blastocyst was implanted during day 24 and explain the advantage of this change.   **2**

Prediction _____

_____

Explanation _____

_____

7. The pedigree chart below shows the inheritance of haemophilia in a family. The allele for haemophilia (h) is sex-linked and recessive to the normal allele (H).

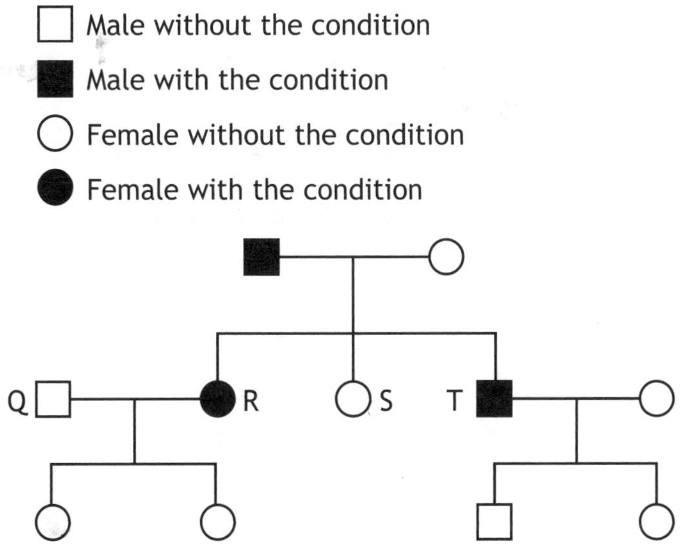

☐ Male without the condition

■ Male with the condition

○ Female without the condition

● Female with the condition

(a) (i) Explain why individual R has haemophilia even although her mother was not affected.   **1**

_____

_____

(ii) Give the genotype of individual S.   **1**

_____

MARKS | DO NOT WRITE IN THIS MARGIN

7. **(continued)**

(b) Individuals Q and R are expecting their third child.

Following the results of an amniocentesis test, the parents are told that their expected baby will be male.

(i) Describe what is meant by amniocentesis and explain how the test can reveal the gender of an unborn baby.

Meaning _____ 1

_____

Explanation _____ 1

_____

(ii) Calculate the percentage chance that the expected male baby of individuals Q and R will have haemophilia.

Space for calculation

_____ % 1

8. The diagram below shows the heart and some of its associated nerves.

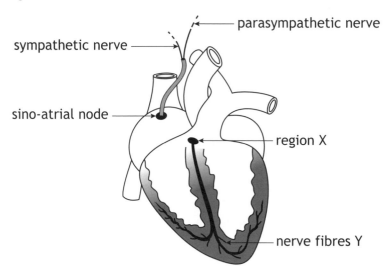

(a) (i) Name the region of the brain which regulates the sino-atrial node (SAN) through the action of the sympathetic and parasympathetic nerves shown. 1

_____

(ii) The sympathetic and parasympathetic nerves act antagonistically.

Explain the meaning of this statement with reference to heart rate. 1

_____

_____

MARKS | DO NOT WRITE IN THIS MARGIN

8. (continued)

(b)   (i) Name region X.   **1**

_____

(ii) Describe the role of region X and nerve fibres Y in the cardiac cycle.   **2**

_____

_____

9. The diagram below show stages in thrombosis within a blood vessel.

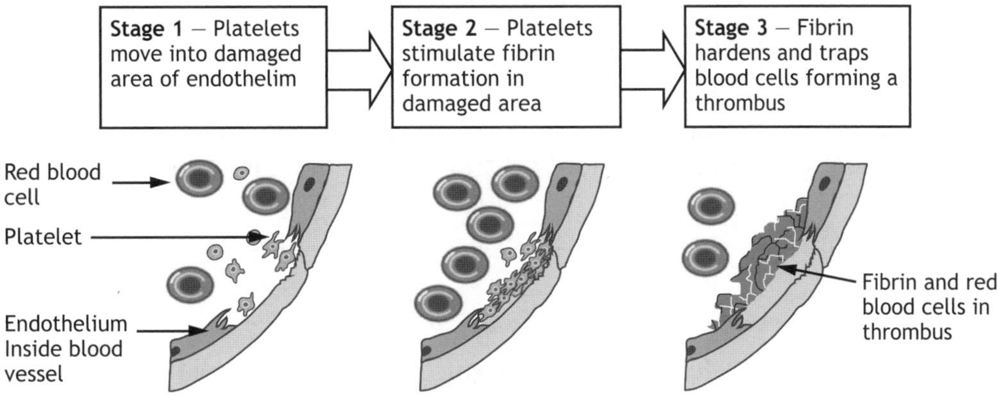

(a) Give an example of how damage to the endothelium can occur.   **1**

_____

_____

(b) Name the soluble protein present in blood plasma from which fibrin is produced.   **1**

_____

(c) Describe how a thrombosis can lead to myocardial infarction (MI).   **2**

_____

_____

_____

MARKS | DO NOT WRITE IN THIS MARGIN

10. The graph below shows changes in the blood glucose concentrations in diabetic and non-diabetic individuals after each had consumed a glucose drink.

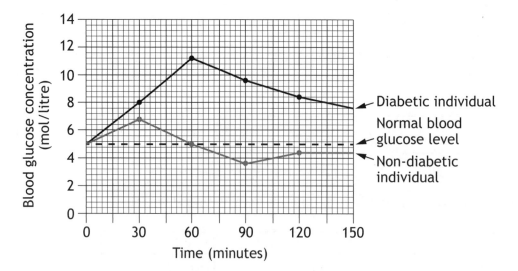

(a) (i) Describe why the blood glucose concentration in the non-diabetic individual increased more slowly than in the diabetic individual. **1**

_____

_____

(ii) Assuming that no further intake of glucose occurred, explain why the blood glucose of the non-diabetic individual increased after 90 minutes. **1**

_____

_____

(b) Give **two** reasons why the blood glucose levels of the diabetic individual decreased after 60 minutes.

1 _____ **1**

2 _____ **1**

(c) Compare insulin production in Type 1 and Type 2 diabetes. **1**

_____

_____

MARKS | DO NOT WRITE IN THIS MARGIN

11. Describe the localisation of brain functions within the cerebrum and the role of the corpus callosum.   4

Space for answer

_____

_____

_____

_____

_____

_____

12. The diagram below shows parts of some cells in the central nervous system (CNS).

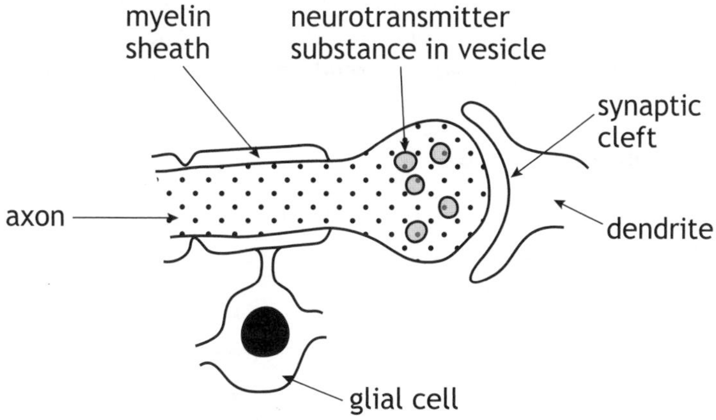

myelin sheath   neurotransmitter substance in vesicle

synaptic cleft

axon

dendrite

glial cell

(a) (i) Describe the function of the myelin sheath.   1

_____

_____

(ii) The specific glial cell shown in the diagram is involved in the production of the myelin sheath.

Give **one** other function of glial cells.   1

_____

_____

MARKS | DO NOT WRITE IN THIS MARGIN

12.   (continued)

(b)   (i)   Describe how neurotransmitters are involved in the passage of nervous impulses across the synapse.   2

_____

_____

_____

(ii)   Name the neurotransmitters involved in reduction of pain intensity following a trauma.   1

_____

13.   In an investigation into the effects of caffeine on learning, thirty 25 year old volunteers were split into three groups of 10 individuals. Members of each group were given different dosages of caffeine as shown in **Table 1** below. Each individual was blindfolded and asked to try a finger maze as shown in the **Diagram** below. The number of errors made during each trial was recorded and each individual completed six trials consecutively with no breaks between trials.

The results are shown in **Table 2** opposite.

Table 1

Group	Caffeine dosage given (mg)
1	50
2	100
3	150

Diagram

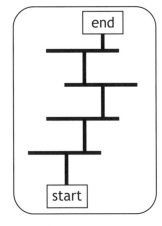

MARKS | DO NOT WRITE IN THIS MARGIN

13. **(continued)**

Table 2

Trial	Average number of errors per group		
	Group 1	Group 2	Group 3
1	7	6	7
2	6	6	6
3	4	3	2
4	2	3	1
5	1	2	0
6	0	0	0

(a) Give a hypothesis that could be tested by this experiment.   1

_____

_____

(b)   (i) Identify the dependent variable in this investigation   1

_____

(ii) Give **one** variable, not already indicated, which would have to be kept constant to ensure valid comparison between the three groups could be made.   1

_____

(c) Describe a suitable control for this experiment.   1

_____

_____

MARKS

13.   (continued)

(d)   (i)   On the grid below, plot line graphs to show **all** of the results of this experiment.   3

(Additional graph paper, if required, can be found on page 79.)

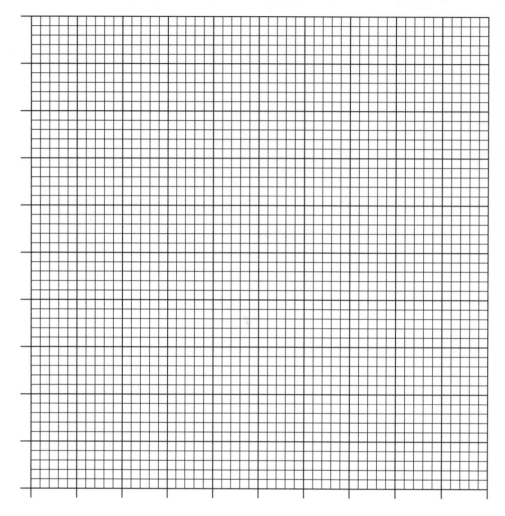

(ii)   Explain why any conclusion drawn from the results of this experiment might not be reliable and suggest an improvement which could increase reliability.

Explanation _____   1

_____

Improvement _____   1

_____

MARKS | DO NOT WRITE IN THIS MARGIN

14. The bacterial species, *Campylobacter*, *Salmonella* and *E coli* 0157 each cause infections of the digestive system that result in vomiting and diarrhoea.

The chart below shows reported number of cases of these infections in a Scottish health board area between 1991 and 1996.

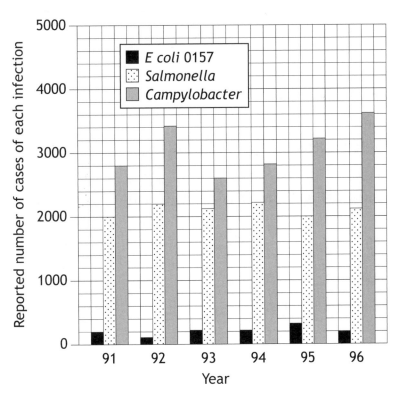

(a) (i) **Use values from the chart** to describe the changes in the numbers of reported cases of *Campylobacter* between 1991 and 1996.   2

_____

_____

_____

(ii) Calculate the percentage increase in the **total** numbers of reported cases of these infections between 1991 and 1996.   1

Space for calculation

_____ %

MARKS DO NOT WRITE IN THIS MARGIN

14. (continued)

(b) Give **two** precautions which can be taken to reduce the number of cases of these infections. **2**

1 ____

2 ____

15. Note that Question 15 contains a choice.

Answer **either A or B** in the space below.

A Describe non-specific defences against disease. **8**

OR

B Describe the roles of T and B lymphocytes in specific immune response to disease. **8**

Space for answer

[END OF MODEL PAPER]

MARKS | DO NOT WRITE IN THIS MARGIN

ADDITIONAL SPACE FOR ANSWERS AND ROUGH WORK

Additional Graph for Question 13 (d) (i).

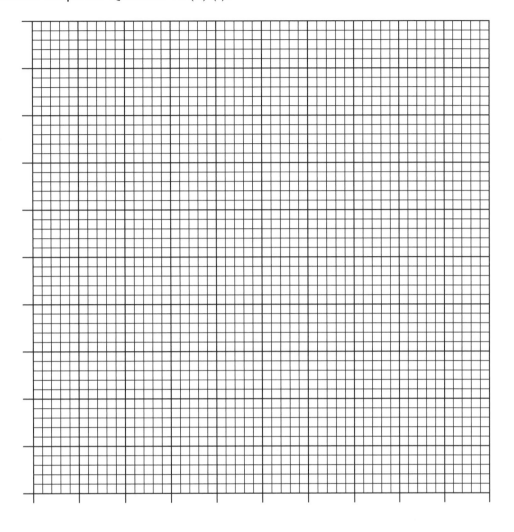

ADDITIONAL SPACE FOR ANSWERS AND ROUGH WORK

ADDITIONAL SPACE FOR ANSWERS AND ROUGH WORK

ADDITIONAL SPACE FOR ANSWERS AND ROUGH WORK

Model Paper 2

Whilst this Model Paper has been specially commissioned by Hodder Gibson for use as practice for the Higher (for Curriculum for Excellence) exams, the key reference documents remain the SQA Specimen Paper 2014 and SQA Past Paper 2015.

National
Qualifications
MODEL PAPER 2

Human Biology
Section 1—Questions

Duration — 2 hours and 30 minutes

Instructions for the completion of Section 1 are given on *Page two* of your question and answer booklet.

Record your answers on the answer grid on *Page three* of your question and answer booklet.

Before leaving the examination room you must give your question and answer booklet to the Invigilator; if you do not, you may lose all the marks for this paper.

HODDER
GIBSON
LEARN MORE

SECTION 1 — 20 marks

Attempt ALL questions

1. Stem cells in bone marrow give rise to

   A   platelets only

   B   red blood cells only

   C   red blood cells and platelets

   D   red blood cells, platelets and phagocytes.

2. The graph below shows changes in the number of human stem cells in a culture. The activity of the enzyme glutaminase present in the cells over an eight-day period is also shown.

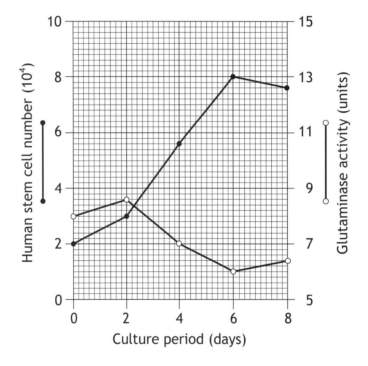

   How many units of glutaminase activity were recorded when the cell number was 50% of its maximum over the eight days?

   A   6

   B   8

   C   9

   D   13

3. Which line in the table below describes correctly aspects of cell division in somatic and germline cells?

	Cell type	Type of cell division	Chromosome complement of daughter cells
A	somatic	mitosis	haploid
B	germline	meiosis	haploid
C	somatic	meiosis	diploid
D	germline	mitosis	haploid

4. The main components of a ribosome are

A   rRNA and tRNA

B   mRNA and protein

C   rRNA and protein

D   mRNA and tRNA.

5. Proteins may be modified after translation before they become functional.

The list below shows changes that could modify protein chains.

1   cutting and combining polypeptide chains

2   adding carbohydrates to the protein chain

3   adding phosphate to the protein chain

Which of these changes are examples of post-translational modification of protein structure?

A   1 and 2 only

B   1 and 3 only

C   2 and 3 only

D   1, 2 and 3

6. Which line in the table below describes correctly fast twitch muscle fibres?

	Main energy storage substance	Relative number of mitochondria compared to slow twitch fibres
A	Fat	Fewer
B	Fat	More
C	Glycogen	Fewer
D	Glycogen	More

7. The graph below shows the concentration of lactic acid in the blood of an athlete and an untrained person during a 20 second period running on a treadmill.

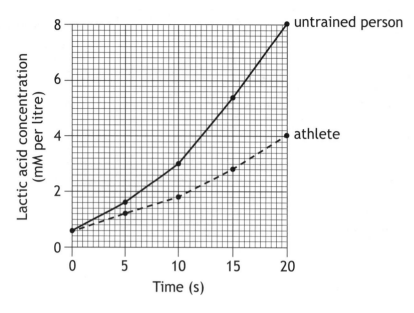

What was the average increase in lactic acid concentration per second in the blood of the athlete over the period?

A   0.170 mM per litre

B   0.200 mM per litre

C   0.375 mM per litre

D   0.400 mM per litre

8. Which line in the table below describes correctly conditions related to the Rhesus factor in which a fetus would be **most** at risk from its mother's immune system?

	Pregnancy	Maternal blood type	Fetal blood type
A	First	Rhesus negative	Rhesus positive
B	Second	Rhesus positive	Rhesus negative
C	Second	Rhesus negative	Rhesus positive
D	First	Rhesus positive	Rhesus negative

9. Cardiac output is calculated using the formula below.

    Cardiac output (l per minute) = *Heart rate* (beats per minute) x *Stroke volume* (cm³)

    The table below shows the cardiac outputs and heart rates of four individuals.

Individual	Cardiac output (l per minute)	Heart rate (beats per minute)
A	5.8	60
B	6.1	68
C	7.2	72
D	7.6	78

    Which individual has the greatest stroke volume?

10. Part of an electrocardiogram (ECG) trace from an individual is shown below.

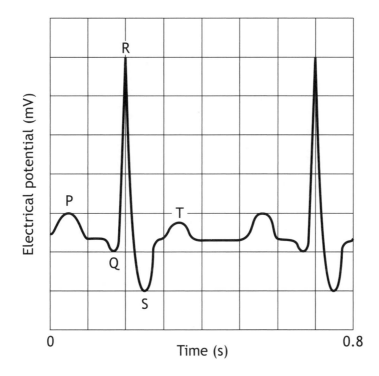

    What is this individual's heart rate?

    A   100 beats per minute

    B   120 beats per minute

    C   150 beats per minute

    D   200 beats per minute

11. The ratio of high density to low density lipoproteins (HDL : LDL) in the blood is related to the level of cholesterol in the blood. Cholesterol level is related to chances of an individual developing atherosclerosis.

    Which line in the table below shows these relationships correctly?

	HDL : LDL	Level of cholesterol in the blood	Chances of developing atherosclerosis
A	High	Low	Decreased
B	High	High	Increased
C	Low	Low	Increased
D	low	High	Decreased

12. The graph below shows how the concentration of insulin in the blood is affected by changes in the concentration of glucose in the blood.

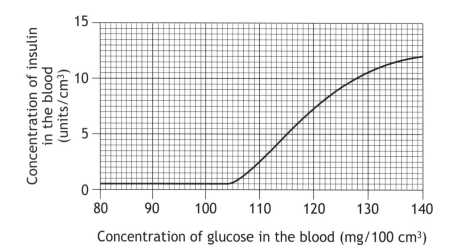

    What is the total mass of glucose present in the blood stream of an individual with 5 litres of blood and an insulin concentration of 5 units per cm^3?

    A   115 mg

    B   575 mg

    C   1150 mg

    D   5750 mg

13. Which line in the table below identifies correctly the hormones which stimulate the inter-conversions between glucose and glycogen?

	glucose → glycogen	glycogen → glucose
A	Insulin	Glucagon and adrenaline
B	Insulin and glucagon	Adrenaline
C	Insulin and adrenaline	Insulin
D	Adrenaline	Insulin and glucagon

14. The pedigree chart below shows the inheritance of albinism in part of a family.

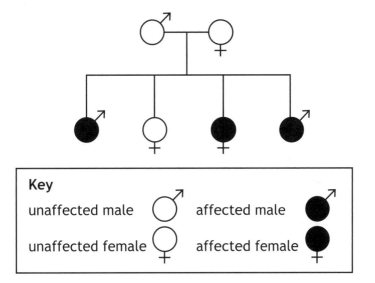

According to information in the chart, albinism is a characteristic which is

A   recessive and autosomal

B   dominant and autosomal

C   recessive and sex-linked

D   dominant and sex-linked.

15. The speed of transmission of an impulse along an axon is enhanced by

A   diffusion of neurotransmitters

B   excitatory signals

C   reverberating neural pathways

D   myelination of the fibre.

16. Which line in the table below matches correctly a neurotransmitter and information related to its functions?

	Neurotransmitter	Function	Function
A	Dopamine	Reduces feeling of pain	Induces feeling of pleasure
B	Endorphin	Reduces feeling of pain	Release of sex hormones
C	Dopamine	Release of sex hormones	Reinforces behaviour in the reward pathway
D	Endorphin	Induces feeling of pleasure	Reinforces behaviour in the reward pathway

17. A volunteer was asked to perform 10 trials of a finger maze. The graph below shows the time taken and the number of errors made in each of the trials.

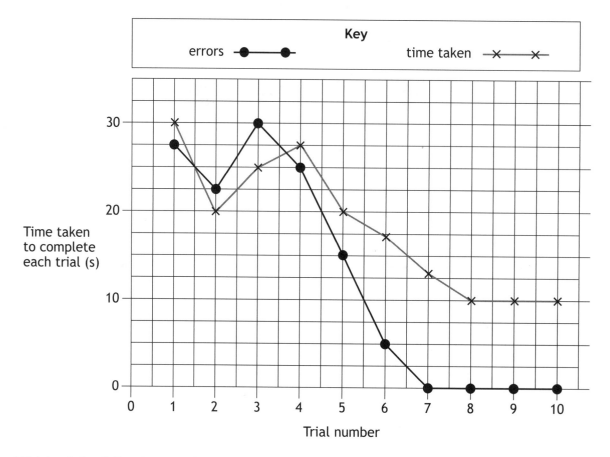

Which of the following conclusions is correct?

A   The fastest time to complete the maze was 4 seconds

B   The time taken for trial 5 was 20 seconds

C   When the number of errors was 10 the time taken was 25 seconds

D   The number of errors steadily decreased as the number of trials increased

18. The pie chart below shows the relative number of deaths from various causes in the population of a developing country.

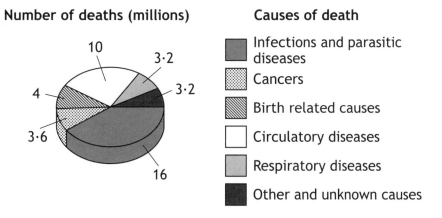

Number of deaths (millions)

Causes of death

■ Infections and parasitic diseases

▦ Cancers

▨ Birth related causes

□ Circulatory diseases

▧ Respiratory diseases

■ Other and unknown causes

What percentage of deaths was due to birth related causes?

A   4%

B   8%

C   10%

D   11%

19. Which of the following describes autoimmunity?

The production of antibodies in response to

A   infection

B   harmless antigens

C   vaccination

D   self antigens.

20. Which line in the table below classifies correctly terms which describe the spread of infectious diseases?

	Regular cases in an area	Occasional cases in an area	Unusually high number of cases in an area	Cases occurring globally
A	Endemic	Sporadic	Epidemic	Pandemic
B	Epidemic	Sporadic	Pandemic	Epidemic
C	Endemic	Epidemic	Sporadic	Pandemic
D	Pandemic	Endemic	Epidemic	Sporadic

[END OF SECTION 1. NOW ATTEMPT THE QUESTIONS IN SECTION 2 OF YOUR QUESTION AND ANSWER BOOKLET]

National
Qualifications
MODEL PAPER 2

Human Biology
Section 1 — Answer Grid and Section 2

Duration — 2 hours and 30 minutes

Fill in these boxes and read what is printed below.

Full name of centre

Town

Forename(s)

Surname

Number of seat

Date of birth

Day	Month	Year
D D	M M	Y Y

Scottish candidate number

Total marks — 100

SECTION 1 — 20 marks

Attempt ALL questions.

Instructions for completion of Section 1 are given on *Page two*.

SECTION 2 — 80 marks

Attempt ALL questions.

Write your answers in the spaces provided. Additional space for answers and rough work is provided at the end of this booklet. If you use this space, write clearly the number of the question you are attempting. Any rough work must be written in this booklet. You should score through your rough work when you have written your fair copy.

Use **blue** or **black** ink.

Before leaving the examination room you must give this booklet to the Invigilator; if you do not, you may lose all the marks for this paper.

HODDER
GIBSON
LEARN MORE

SECTION 1— 20 marks

The questions for Section 1 are contained on *Page 85*.
Read these and record your answers on the answer grid on *Page three* opposite.
Do NOT use gel pens.

1. The answer to each question is **either** A, B, C or D. Decide what your answer is, then fill in the appropriate bubble (see sample question below).

2. There is **only one correct** answer to each question.

3. Any rough working should be done on the additional space for answers and rough work at the end of this booklet.

Sample Question

The digestive enzyme pepsin is most active in the

    A   mouth

    B   stomach

    C   duodenum

    D   pancreas.

The correct answer is **B**—stomach. The answer **B** bubble has been clearly filled in (see below).

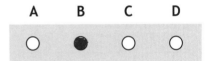

Changing an answer

If you decide to change your answer, cancel your first answer by putting a cross through it (see below) and fill in the answer you want. The answer below has been changed to **D**.

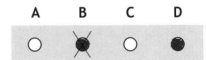

If you then decide to change back to an answer you have already scored out, put a tick (✓) to the **right** of the answer you want, as shown below:

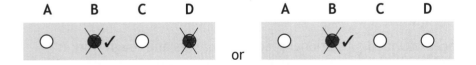

SECTION 1 — Answer Grid

	A	B	C	D
1	○	○	○	○
2	○	○	○	○
3	○	○	○	○
4	○	○	○	○
5	○	○	○	○
6	○	○	○	○
7	○	○	○	○
8	○	○	○	○
9	○	○	○	○
10	○	○	○	○
11	○	○	○	○
12	○	○	○	○
13	○	○	○	○
14	○	○	○	○
15	○	○	○	○
16	○	○	○	○
17	○	○	○	○
18	○	○	○	○
19	○	○	○	○
20	○	○	○	○

MARKS | DO NOT WRITE IN THIS MARGIN

SECTION 2 — 80 marks

Attempt ALL questions

Note that question 15 contains a choice.

1. The diagram below shows part of a DNA molecule during replication and other molecules associated with it.

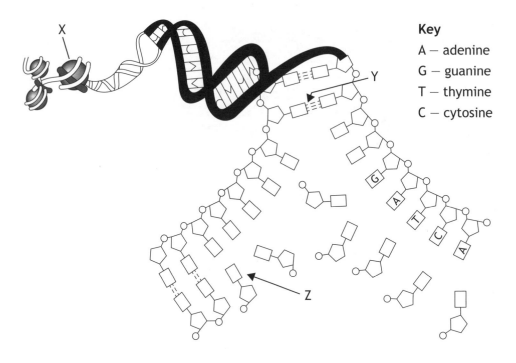

Key
A — adenine
G — guanine
T — thymine
C — cytosine

(a) Name molecule X which is associated with the tightly coiled DNA.   1

_____

(b) Name the type of bond shown at Y.   1

_____

(c) Name base Z.   1

_____

(d) <u>Underline</u> one word in each pair to make the sentence correct.   1

DNA is a double stranded {parallel/antiparallel} molecule with deoxyribose and a {base/phosphate} at the 3′ and 5′ ends of each strand respectively.

MARKS | DO NOT WRITE IN THIS MARGIN

2. The graph below shows how temperature changed during one cycle of the polymerase chain reaction (PCR).

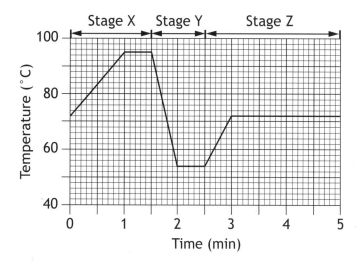

(a) (i) Calculate the range of temperature that the PCR reaction tube experiences during one cycle of PCR.   1

Space for calculation

_____ °C

(ii) Describe what happens to the DNA during stage X.   1

_____

_____

(iii) Short sections of DNA called primers are involved in Stage Y.

State what happens to these primers during Stage Y.   1

_____

_____

MARKS DO NOT WRITE IN THIS MARGIN

2. (a) (continued)

   (iv) Suggest why the temperature is increased during Stage Z.   **1**

   _____

   _____

   (b) Give **one** application of PCR.   **1**

   _____

   _____

3. Give an account of tumour production by cancer cells.   **4**

   _____

   _____

   _____

   _____

   _____

   _____

   _____

   _____

   _____

   _____

   _____

MARKS | DO NOT WRITE IN THIS MARGIN

4. Hydrogen peroxide is a toxic chemical which is produced in human metabolism.

Catalase is an enzyme that breaks down hydrogen peroxide as shown below.

$$\text{hydrogen peroxide} \xrightarrow{\text{catalase}} \text{water + oxygen}$$

Experiments were carried out to investigate how changing the concentration of catalase affects the rate of hydrogen peroxide breakdown.

Filter paper discs were soaked in catalase solutions of different concentration.

Each disc was then added to a beaker of hydrogen peroxide solution as shown in the **diagram** below.

The disc sank to the bottom of the beaker before rising back up to the surface.

The time taken for each disc to rise to the surface was used to measure the reaction rates.

The results of the investigation are shown in the **table** below.

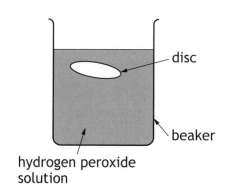

hydrogen peroxide solution

Catalase concentration (%)	Average time for ten discs to rise (s)
0·125	9·8
0·5	5·0
1·0	3·8
2·0	3·8

(a) Explain why the filter paper discs rose to the surface of the hydrogen peroxide solution.

1

_____

_____

MARKS | DO NOT WRITE IN THIS MARGIN

4. **(continued)**

(b) (i) Give the dependent variable in this experiment.   **1**

_____

(ii) Give **two** variables that should be controlled during this investigation.   **2**

1 _____

2 _____

(c) Describe **one** feature of this investigation which makes the results more reliable.   **1**

_____

_____

(d) It was suggested that the filter paper itself was reacting with the hydrogen peroxide.

Describe how this suggestion could be confirmed using the same type of procedure.   **1**

_____

_____

MARKS | DO NOT WRITE IN THIS MARGIN

4. (continued)

(e) Plot a line graph to show the results of the investigation.   **2**

(Additional graph paper, if required, can be found on page 120.)

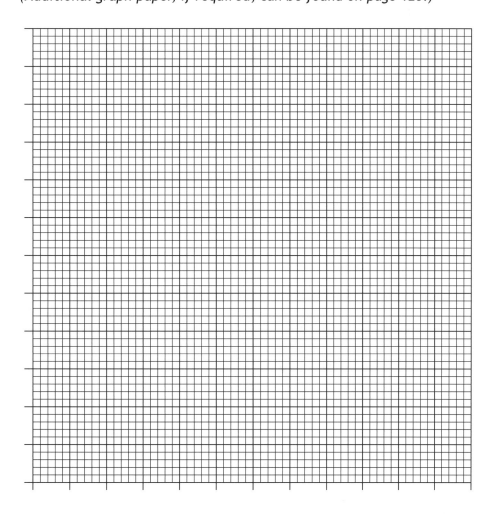

(f) State **two** conclusions that can be drawn from these results.   **2**

1 _____

_____

2 _____

_____

MARKS | DO NOT WRITE IN THIS MARGIN

5. The diagram below shows parts of two stages in the aerobic respiration of glucose.

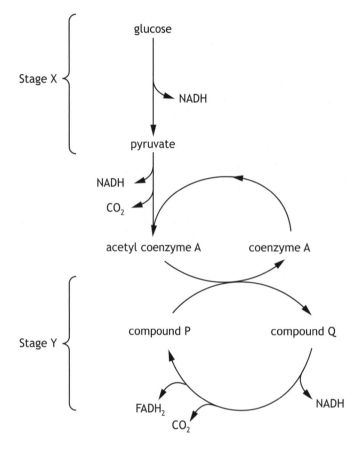

(a) Name stages X and Y.   **1**

X _____

Y _____

(b) Name compounds P and Q.   **1**

P _____

Q _____

(c) Describe the role of dehydrogenase enzymes in stages X and Y.   **1**

_____

_____

MARKS | DO NOT WRITE IN THIS MARGIN

5.   (continued)

(d) The diagram below shows part of the electron transport chain attached to the inner membrane of a mitochondrion.

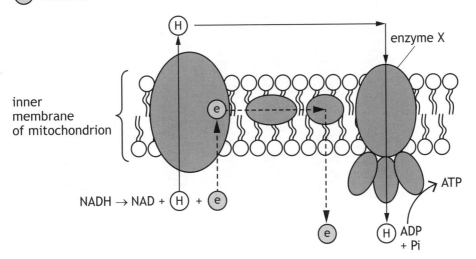

(i)   In this system, hydrogen ions are pumped across the inner mitochondrial membrane as shown in the diagram.

Describe the source of energy required for this process.   1

_____

(ii) The return flow of hydrogen ions drives enzyme X which results in the production of ATP.

Name enzyme X.   1

_____

MARKS | DO NOT WRITE IN THIS MARGIN

6. The graph below shows information relating to the occurrence of high blood pressure in British men of different ages.

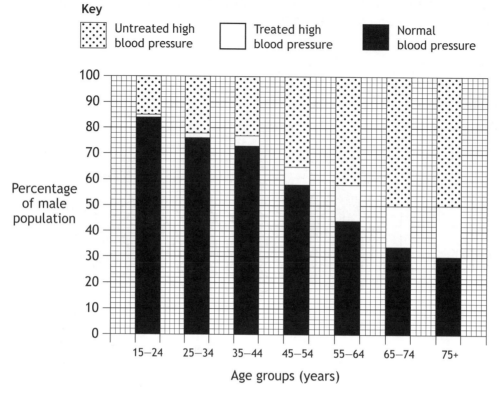

Key

▦ Untreated high blood pressure   ☐ Treated high blood pressure   ■ Normal blood pressure

(a) State the percentage of British men aged between 25 and 34 that have high blood pressure.

1

_____ %

(b) Calculate the simplest whole number ratio of the percentage of men aged between 55 – 64 with treated high blood pressure to those untreated individuals.

1

Space for calculation

_____ : _____

      treated   untreated

Page twelve

MARKS | DO NOT WRITE IN THIS MARGIN

6. (continued)

(c) Describe **one** trend shown by the graph and suggest an explanation for it.   1

Trend _____

Explanation _____

7. The diagrams below represent gamete production in an ovary and part of a testis.

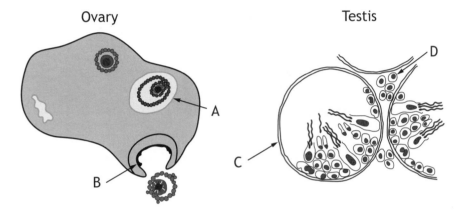

Ovary   Testis

(a) Name structures A and B.

A _____   1

B _____   1

(b) Name structure C and describe its role in reproduction.

Name _____   1

Role _____   1

_____

(c) Name a hormone produced by cell D.   1

_____

MARKS | DO NOT WRITE IN THIS MARGIN

8. Analysis of current fertility rates can be used to predict population change in the future.

Graph 1 shows the number of children born to a sample of twenty British women of reproductive age. The sample was taken in 2000.

Graph 1

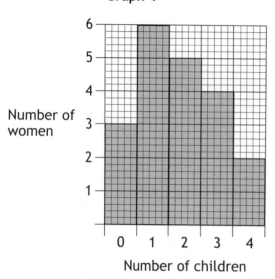

Number of women (y-axis)

Number of children (x-axis)

(a) Fertility rate for a country is calculated by dividing the total number of children in a sample by the number of women in the sample.

   (i) From **Graph 1**, calculate the fertility rate of this sample. 1

   Space for calculation

_____

   (ii) State how the calculation of the fertility rate for this country could be made more reliable. 1

   _____

   _____

MARKS | DO NOT WRITE IN THIS MARGIN

8. **(continued)**

Graph 2 shows the predicted population changes in the UK for four different fertility rates.

Graph 2

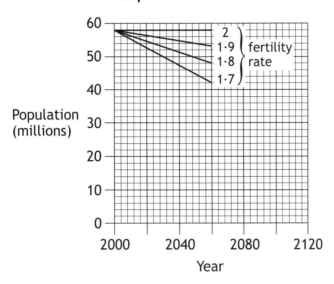

(b) Predict the population of the **UK** in 2100 based on a fertility rate of 1.7.   1

_____

(c) In a sample of twenty families in Thailand, a developing country, three women have two children, ten women have three children and seven women have four children.

Calculate the fertility rate for this sample.   1

Space for calculation

_____

(d) Explain how chemical contraceptives based on synthetic hormones work.   1

_____

_____

MARKS | DO NOT WRITE IN THIS MARGIN

9. Rising levels of obesity are a major concern in modern Scottish society.

Successive governments have tried to promote healthy eating and exercise in an attempt to address this problem.

(a)   (i)   One measure of obesity is the body mass index (BMI).

State the measurements required to calculate BMI.   **1**

_____

_____

(ii)   State the minimum value of BMI that is generally used to indicate that an individual is obese.   **1**

_____

(b)   Describe how exercise reduces the risk of an individual becoming obese.   **1**

_____

_____

_____

(c)   State two ways that exercise reduces the risk factors for cardiovascular disease (CVD).

1_____   **1**

_____

2_____   **1**

_____

MARKS | DO NOT WRITE IN THIS MARGIN

10. The image below shows a vertical section through a human brain.

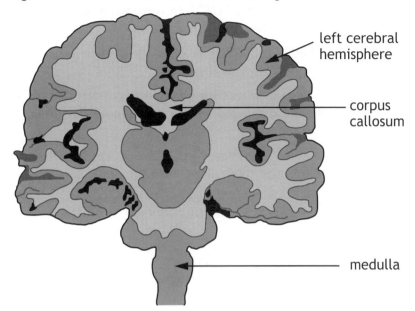

left cerebral hemisphere

corpus callosum

medulla

(a) State the function of the motor area in the left cerebral hemisphere.   1

_____

_____

(b) State the function of the corpus callosum.   1

_____

_____

(c) (i) Name the division of the nervous system with centres in the medulla.   1

_____

   (ii) Describe how this division of the nervous system controls heart rate.   1

_____

_____

_____

MARKS | DO NOT WRITE IN THIS MARGIN

11. An investigation was carried out into the influence of adult behaviour on the behaviour of young children. Some groups of children watched a recording of either a man or a woman being aggressive towards a cloth doll.

Other groups of children watched a recording of either a man or a woman behaving in a non-aggressive manner towards the doll.

Each of the children was then placed in a room on their own with the doll. The number of aggressive acts they displayed over a five minute period was counted.

The figures in the table below show the average number of aggressive acts that the children displayed while in the room alone with the doll.

Gender of children	Recorded adult behaviour previously observed by children			
	Aggressive man	Aggressive woman	Non-aggressive man	Non-aggressive woman
	Average number of aggressive acts displayed by the children			
Boys	18.7	7.9	1.0	0.6
Girls	4.4	9.2	0.2	0.8

(a) (i) State the adult and child combination which resulted in the least aggression.   1

_____

(ii) Calculate the percentage increase in aggressive acts displayed by boys when they observed an aggressive man rather than a non-aggressive man.   1

Space for calculation

_____ %

(iii) State a conclusion that can be drawn from these results regarding the part played by the gender of the aggressive adult in determining the behaviour of the children.   1

_____

_____

MARKS | DO NOT WRITE IN THIS MARGIN

11.   (continued)

(b) The children are observing and then repeating the acts of adults.
     Name this form of learning.   1

_____

(c) Suggest a control that could have been used in this investigation.   1

_____

_____

12. The diagram below shows two different neural pathways.

The arrows indicate the direction of the nerve impulses.

Pathway A

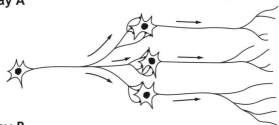

Pathway B

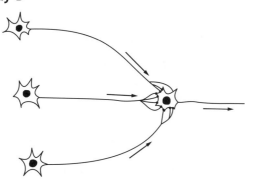

(a) Name the types of pathway represented by A and B.   1

A _____

B _____

(b) Pathways like A are involved in the complex function of the human hand.
     Explain how pathways like A control the function of the hand.   2

_____

_____

_____

MARKS | DO NOT WRITE IN THIS MARGIN

12. (continued)

(c) Neurotransmitters are secreted into synaptic clefts to allow nervous impulses to cross.

Give **one** way in which the neurotransmitters are removed to prevent continuous stimulation of post synaptic neurons.

1

_____

_____

13. The diagram below shows the structure of one strain of the influenza virus.

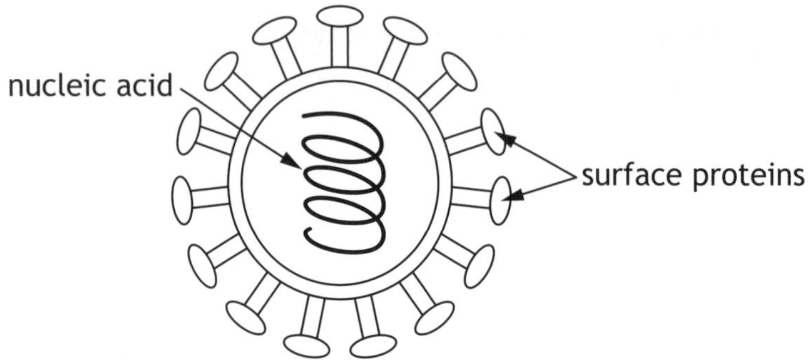

(a) This virus can be used to prepare an influenza vaccine.

To do this the viral nucleic acid must be broken up to prevent the virus replicating but viral surface proteins must be left intact.

Explain why it is necessary to leave the surface proteins intact.

1

_____

_____

(b) A different vaccine is required against each different strain of the influenza virus.

Explain why different vaccines are required.

1

_____

_____

MARKS | DO NOT WRITE IN THIS MARGIN

13. (continued)

(c) Clinical trials of the new vaccine against influenza have shown that it increases the activity of T-lymphocytes in the body.

Describe **two** ways in which T-lymphocytes combat infection.

1 _____   **1**

_____

2 _____   **1**

_____

(d) Clinical trials of vaccines use randomised, placebo-controlled protocols.

Describe how these protocols are set up.   **2**

_____

_____

_____

_____

MARKS | DO NOT WRITE IN THIS MARGIN

14. The **Graph** below shows the number of reported cases of hospital acquired infections (HAI) in a particular hospital over a period of 7 years, during which time the overall number of patients remained constant.

The **Table** below shows the percentage of cases of HAI in the hospital attributed to two types of bacteria, *Clostridium* and *Staphylococcus* over the same 7 year period.

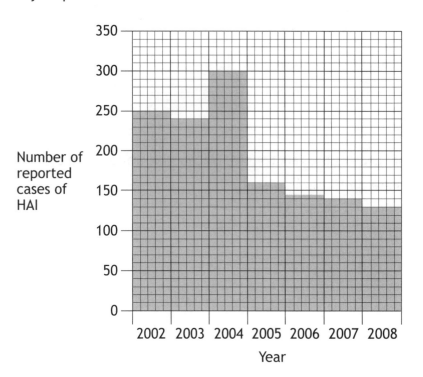

Bacterial types	Percentage of cases of HAI in each year attributed to bacterial types (%)						
	2002	2003	2004	2005	2006	2007	2008
Clostridium	32	30	30	51	54	57	59
Staphylococcus	34	32	33	30	31	33	33

(a) From the **Graph**, give the year in which the greatest decrease in total number of cases of HAI occurred, compared with the previous year.   1

_____

MARKS | DO NOT WRITE IN THIS MARGIN

14. (continued)

(b) Use information from the **Graph** to calculate the percentage increase in reported cases of HAI between 2003 and 2004.   1

Space for calculation

_____

(c) In January 2005, a new hand washing procedure was introduced at the hospital.

Predict the effect this procedure would have on the number of reported cases of HAI in 2009.   1

Give a reason for your answer.

Prediction _____

_____

Reason _____

_____

(d) Using the **Graph** and the **Table**, calculate the number of cases of HAI caused by *Staphylococcus* in 2005.   1

Space for calculation

_____ cases

MARKS | DO NOT WRITE IN THIS MARGIN

14. (continued)

(e) Use the information in the **Table** to compare the **overall** trend in the percentage of *Clostridium* cases over the 7 year period with that of *Staphylococcus* cases. **1**

____

____

(f) Using the **Graph** and the **Table**, draw a conclusion about the effectiveness of the hand washing procedure against *Staphylococcus* and justify your answer.

Conclusion ______________________________________ **1**

____

Justification ____________________________________ **1**

____

MARKS | DO NOT WRITE IN THIS MARGIN

15. **Note that Question 15 contains a choice.**

Answer **either A or B** in the space below.

A   Discuss procedures that can be used to treat infertility.   **8**

OR

B   Discuss the screening and testing procedures which may be carried out as part of antenatal care.   **8**

Space for answer

[END OF MODEL PAPER]

MARKS | DO NOT WRITE IN THIS MARGIN

ADDITIONAL SPACE FOR ANSWERS AND ROUGH WORK

Additional Graph for Question 4 (e)

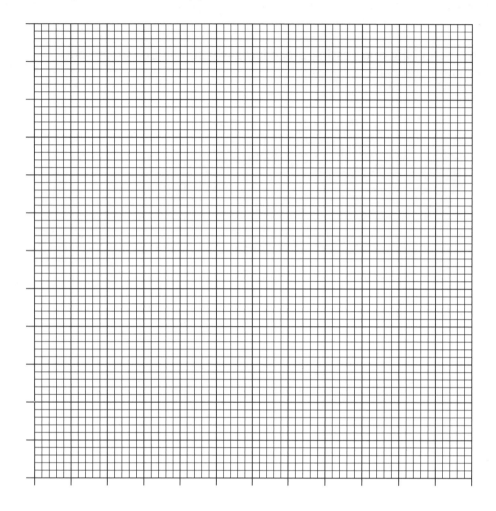

MARKS | DO NOT WRITE IN THIS MARGIN

ADDITIONAL SPACE FOR ANSWERS AND ROUGH WORK

MARKS | DO NOT WRITE IN THIS MARGIN

ADDITIONAL SPACE FOR ANSWERS AND ROUGH WORK

Page twenty-eight

Model Paper 3

Whilst this Model Paper has been specially commissioned by Hodder Gibson for use as practice for the Higher (for Curriculum for Excellence) exams, the key reference documents remain the SQA Specimen Paper 2014 and SQA Past Paper 2015.

National
Qualifications
MODEL PAPER 3

Human Biology
Section 1—Questions

Duration — 2 hours and 30 minutes

Instructions for the completion of Section 1 are given on *Page two* of your question and answer booklet.

Record your answers on the answer grid on *Page three* of your question and answer booklet.

Before leaving the examination room you must give your question and answer booklet to the Invigilator; if you do not, you may lose all the marks for this paper.

SECTION 1 — 20 marks

Attempt ALL questions

1. A DNA molecule contained 8000 nucleotides of which 20% contained adenine.

    How many nucleotides in this molecule would contain guanine?

    A   1600

    B   2400

    C   3200

    D   4800

2. The table below contains statements which may be true or false with regard to DNA replication and mRNA synthesis.

    Which line in the table is fully correct?

	Statement	DNA replication	mRNA synthesis
A	Occurs in the nucleus	true	false
B	Involved in protein synthesis	true	true
C	Require free nucleotides	true	true
D	Involves specific base pairing	false	true

3. Which line in the table below shows correctly the effects of different gene mutations on the protein formed?

	Gene mutation		
	Nonsense	Missense	Frameshift
A	Shortened protein formed	Protein contain one changed amino acid	All amino acids in protein changed from point of mutation
B	Shortened protein formed	All amino acids in protein changed from point of mutation	Protein contain one changed amino acid
C	Protein contain one changed amino acid	Shortened protein formed	All amino acids in protein changed from point of mutation
D	All amino acids in protein changed from point of mutation	Shortened protein formed	Protein contain one changed amino acid

4. The diagram below shows a section of chromosome and the positions of ten genes before and after a mutation.

before | 1 2 3 4 5 6 7 8 9 10 |

after | 1 2 3 4 5 6 7 8 6 7 8 9 10 |

The type of mutation involved in this example is

A   deletion

B   translocation

C   duplication

D   inversion.

5. The diagram below shows a branched metabolic pathway.

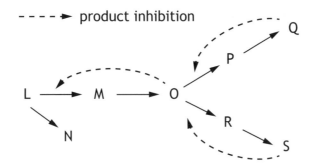

Which reaction would occur if substances Q and S were present in high concentrations?

A   L → M

B   R → S

C   O → P

D   L → N

6. Liver tissue contains an enzyme which breaks down alcohol. The graph below shows the effect of copper ions on the breakdown of alcohol by this enzyme over a 30-minute period.

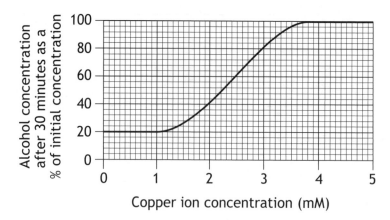

Which of the following conclusions can be drawn from the graph?

A   4.5mM copper has no effect on enzyme activity

B   2.5mM copper halves the enzyme activity

C   0.5nM copper completely inhibits enzyme activity

D   Increasing copper from 1mM to 3mM increases enzyme activity

7. In an investigation into the effects of ATP on muscle fibre contraction, pieces of muscle measuring 50mm were placed into 1% ATP solutions and their lengths measured after 5 minutes of immersion.

    Which of the following would make the best control for this investigation?

    Pieces of muscle fibre

A   in glucose solution

B   in distilled water

C   in 2% ATP solution

D   left out of any solution.

8. The diagram below illustrates the hormonal control of a 30-day menstrual cycle.

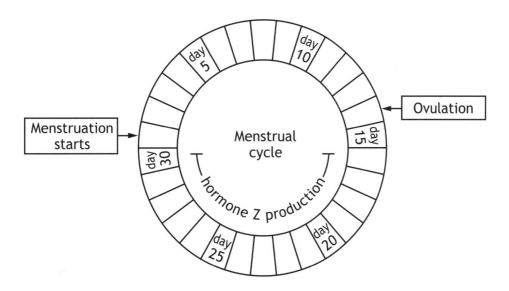

Which line of the table below identifies correctly hormone Z and the structure which produces this hormone?

	Hormone Z	Structure which produces hormone Z
A	Oestrogen	Follicle
B	Oestrogen	Corpus luteum
C	Progesterone	Follicle
D	Progesterone	Corpus luteum

9. The following procedures can be used in the treatment of infertility.

1   artificial insemination

2   intracytoplasmic sperm injection

3   pre-implantation genetic screening

Which of these procedures require *in vitro* fertilisation (IVF) as part of the fertility treatment?

A   1 and 2

B   2 and 3

C   1 and 3

D   1, 2 and 3

10. The diagram below shows a section through the heart.

     At which point would the sino-atrial node (SAN) be found?

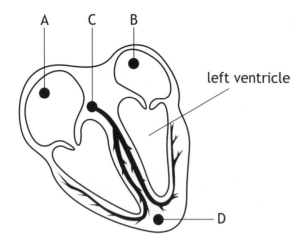

11. The average duration of diastole and systole in a hospital patient over a period of time were measured and are shown below.

     diastole   = 0.3 seconds

     atrial systole   = 0.1s

     ventricular systole = 0.2 seconds

     What was the average heart rate of this individual over the period of time?

     A   60 beats per minute

     B   72 beats per minute

     C   100 beats per minute

     D   120 beats per minute

12. The diagram below shows part of the mechanism which controls ovulation.

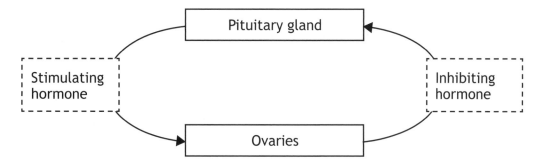

Which line in the table below identifies correctly the hormones in the diagram?

	Stimulating hormone	Inhibiting hormone
A	FSH	Oestrogen
B	FSH	LH
C	Progesterone	LH
D	Progesterone	Oestrogen

13. The pedigree diagram below shows the inheritance of the Rhesus D antigen through three generations of a family. The allele coding for the presence of the Rhesus D antigen is autosomal dominant.

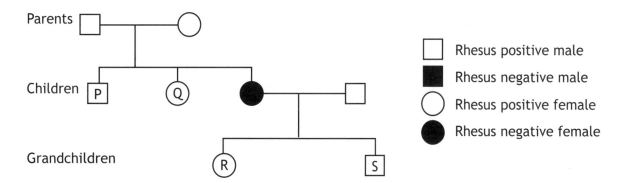

Which of the individuals in the pedigree diagram **must** be heterozygous?

A   P, Q, R and S

B   P and Q only

C   R and S only

D   Q and R only

14. The diagram below shows the stages of development during which major or minor malformations of certain organs may occur if there is exposure to nicotine.

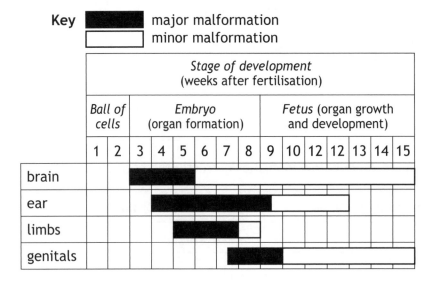

| Key | ■ major malformation |
| --- | □ minor malformation |

	Stage of development (weeks after fertilisation)														
	Ball of cells		Embryo (organ formation)						Fetus (organ growth and development)						
	1	2	3	4	5	6	7	8	9	10	12	12	13	14	15
brain															
ear															
limbs															
genitals															

For how many weeks after fertilisation is there risk of major malformations to these organs?

A   6

B   7

C   9

D   13

15. The diagram below represents a neural pathway.

Stimulus   Response

The type of pathway shown here is a

A   diverging pathway

B   sensory pathway

C   converging pathway

D   reverberating pathway.

16. The diagram below show a vertical section of the human brain.

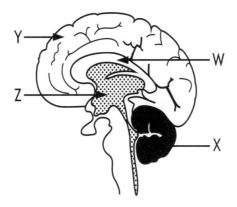

Which line in the table below identifies correctly the function of two areas of the brain?

	Communication between cerebral hemispheres	Reasoning
A	W	X
B	X	Y
C	W	Y
D	Z	W

17. Which of the following structures carries a nervous impulse towards the cell body of a neuron?

A   dendrite

B   axon

C   myelin sheath

D   glial cell

18. In a clinical trial of a new vaccine, volunteers were split into two groups A and B.

Each group contained individuals matched on their age profiles.

Group A was given injections of the new vaccine and Group B was given injections of sugar solution.

Which of the following protocols was involved in this example?

A   placebo control

B   pedigree analysis

C   double-blind procedure

D   randomised treatments

19. On which of the following does the herd immunity threshold **not** depend?

   A   Type of disease

   B   Population density

   C   Effectiveness of vaccine

   D   Quarantine of non-affected individuals

20. The table below contains information about the number of cases of influenza in a health board area over a five-year period.

Year	Influenza cases in January	Influenza cases in July
2001	580	120
2002	620	345
2003	1200	350
2004	120	145
2005	400	100

Which conclusion can be drawn from the information in the table?

   A   There are always more cases of influenza in January than in July

   B   The number of influenza cases in January increased steadily from 2001 until 2005

   C   The average number of influenza cases in January was 212

   D   The number of cases of influenza decreased by 75% between January and July 2005

**[END OF SECTION 1. NOW ATTEMPT THE QUESTIONS IN SECTION 2
OF YOUR QUESTION AND ANSWER BOOKLET]**

National
Qualifications
MODEL PAPER 3

Human Biology
Section 1 — Answer Grid
and Section 2

Duration — 2 hours and 30 minutes

Fill in these boxes and read what is printed below.

Full name of centre

Town

Forename(s)

Surname

Number of seat

Date of birth
Day   Month   Year

Scottish candidate number

Total marks — 100

SECTION 1 — 20 marks

Attempt ALL questions.

Instructions for completion of Section 1 are given on *Page two*.

SECTION 2 — 80 marks

Attempt ALL questions.

Write your answers in the spaces provided. Additional space for answers and rough work is provided at the end of this booklet. If you use this space, write clearly the number of the question you are attempting. Any rough work must be written in this booklet. You should score through your rough work when you have written your fair copy.

Use **blue** or **black** ink.

Before leaving the examination room you must give this booklet to the Invigilator; if you do not, you may lose all the marks for this paper.

SECTION 1— 20 marks

The questions for Section 1 are contained on *Page 125*.
Read these and record your answers on the answer grid on *Page three* opposite.
Do NOT use gel pens.

1. The answer to each question is **either** A, B, C or D. Decide what your answer is, then fill in the appropriate bubble (see sample question below).

2. There is **only one correct** answer to each question.

3. Any rough working should be done on the additional space for answers and rough work at the end of this booklet.

Sample Question

The digestive enzyme pepsin is most active in the

     A   mouth

     B   stomach

     C   duodenum

     D   pancreas.

The correct answer is **B**—stomach. The answer **B** bubble has been clearly filled in (see below).

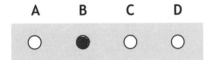

Changing an answer

If you decide to change your answer, cancel your first answer by putting a cross through it (see below) and fill in the answer you want. The answer below has been changed to **D**.

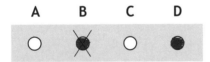

If you then decide to change back to an answer you have already scored out, put a tick (✓) to the **right** of the answer you want, as shown below:

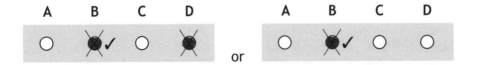

or

SECTION 1 — Answer Grid

	A	B	C	D
1	○	○	○	○
2	○	○	○	○
3	○	○	○	○
4	○	○	○	○
5	○	○	○	○
6	○	○	○	○
7	○	○	○	○
8	○	○	○	○
9	○	○	○	○
10	○	○	○	○
11	○	○	○	○
12	○	○	○	○
13	○	○	○	○
14	○	○	○	○
15	○	○	○	○
16	○	○	○	○
17	○	○	○	○
18	○	○	○	○
19	○	○	○	○
20	○	○	○	○

MARKS | DO NOT WRITE IN THIS MARGIN

SECTION 2 — 80 marks

Attempt ALL questions

Note that question 15 contains a choice.

1. (a) The table below shows information about cells and cell division in the body.

Complete the table.   **2**

Cell type	Type of cell division	Daughter cell type
		Somatic cells
	Mitosis	Germline cells
Germline		Haploid gametes

(b) Identify **three** types of cell formed by the process of cellular differentiation of tissue stem cells in the bone marrow.   **2**

1 _____

2 _____

3 _____

2. The diagram below shows the synthesis of a polypeptide in a cell.

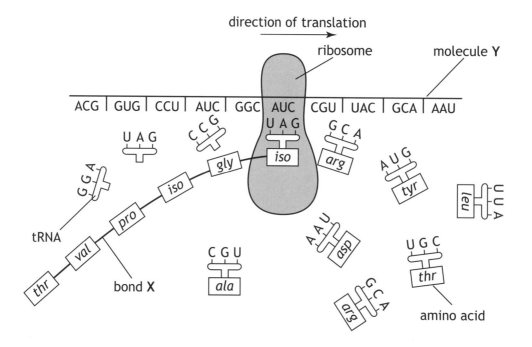

MARKS | DO NOT WRITE IN THIS MARGIN

2. (continued)

(a) Name bond X and molecule Y.

Bond X _____   1

Molecule Y _____   1

(b) Using information from the diagram, complete the boxes below to show the next four amino acids which will be added to complete the polypeptide chain.   1

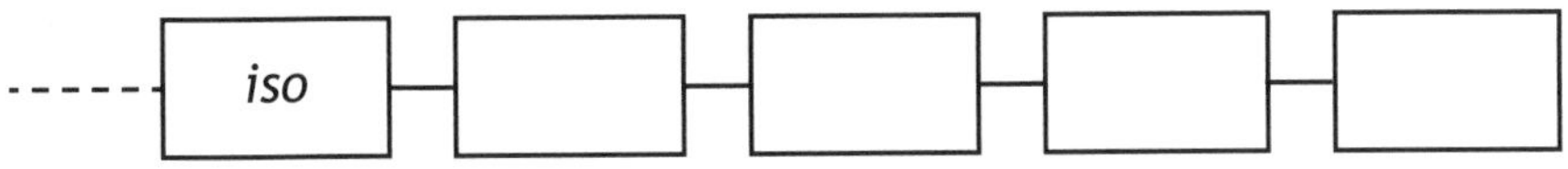

- - - - - | iso |—| | —| | —| | —| |

(c) Give the DNA triplet which codes for the amino acid shown as *thr*.   1

_____

(d) Once completed a polypeptide chain may undergo post translational modification.

Describe an example of a post translational modification of a polypeptide.   1

_____

_____

MARKS | DO NOT WRITE IN THIS MARGIN

3. The diagram below shows parts of the respiration pathway in a cell.

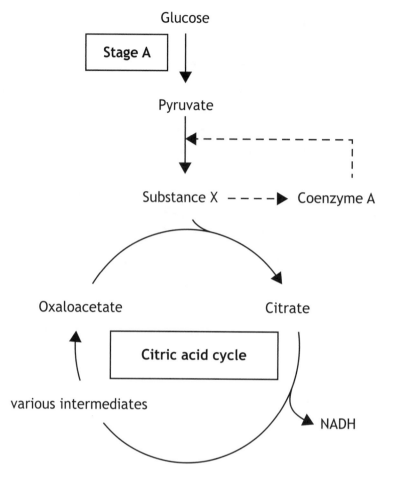

(a) Name stage A and identify the region of a cell in which it occurs.   2

A _____

Region _____

(b) Name substance X.   1

_____

(c) The enzyme phosphofructokinase catalyses a reaction in Stage A.
State how the activity of this enzyme is regulated.   1

_____

_____

(d) Describe how hydrogen carried by NAD is involved in the synthesis of ATP in the electron transport chain.   1

_____

_____

MARKS | DO NOT WRITE IN THIS MARGIN

4. The diagram below shows the evolutionary relationships and origins of humans and some other species.

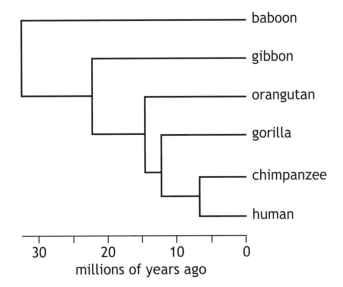

(a) (i) Describe the molecular evidence which allows diagrams such as this to be constructed.   1

_____

(ii) Estimate how long ago the last common ancestor of humans and orangutans existed.   1

_____ million years ago

(b) Explain how the analysis of individual genomes may lead to personalised medicine.   1

_____

_____

_____

MARKS | DO NOT WRITE IN THIS MARGIN

5. The chart below shows how the percentages of slow twitch and fast twitch fibres found in the muscles of athletes varies with the distance of the event for which they train.

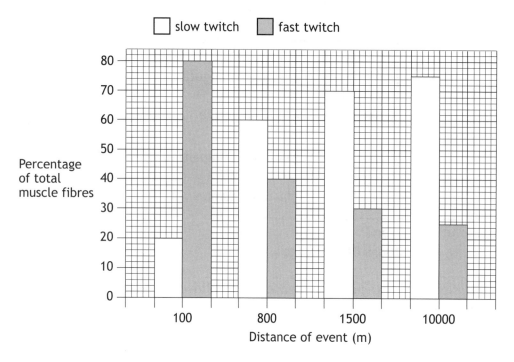

□ slow twitch   ▦ fast twitch

(a) (i) Compare the trends shown in the chart.   1

_____

_____

_____

     (ii) Express the percentage of slow twitch to fast twitch fibres found in the muscles of the 10 000 metres runner as a simple whole number ratio.   1

          Space for calculation

          _____ : _____

             slow twitch   fast twitch

(b) Describe one functional and one structural difference between slow and fast twitch fibres.

     Functional difference _____   1

     Structural difference _____   1

MARKS | DO NOT WRITE IN THIS MARGIN

6. As part of a series of clinical trials, the systolic and diastolic blood pressures of six young adult participants were measured. Each participant was asked to drink 500 cm³ of an energy drink and their blood pressures were measured again one hour after taking the drink.

The results are shown in the table below.

Participant	Initial blood pressure (mm Hg)		Blood pressure one hour after taking the drink (mm Hg)	
	systolic	diastolic	systolic	diastolic
1	120	75	134	82
2	127	80	145	84
3	118	70	124	72
4	134	81	143	83
5	122	73	133	77
6	129	83	137	88
Average reading	125	77	136	81

(a) Calculate the percentage increase in the diastolic pressure of participant 2 one hour after taking the energy drink.   1

Space for calculation

_____ %

(b) (i) Give the dependent variable for this investigation.   1

_____

(ii) Identify **one** variable, not already mentioned, which would have to be kept constant during this investigation.   1

_____

(c) Describe an appropriate control for this investigation.   1

_____

_____

MARKS | DO NOT WRITE IN THIS MARGIN

6. **(continued)**

(d) On the grid provided draw a bar chart to show all the average blood pressure readings shown in the table.   **2**

(Additional graph paper, if required, can be found on page 156.)

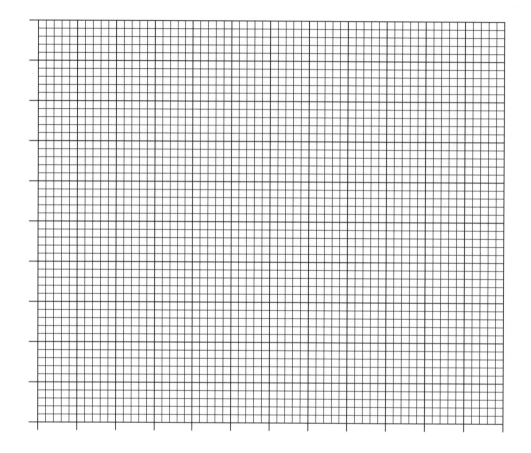

(e) (i) Give **one** conclusion which could be drawn from the results in the table.   **1**

_____

_____

(ii) Suggest why conclusions from these results might not be reliable.   **1**

_____

_____

MARKS | DO NOT WRITE IN THIS MARGIN

6.   (continued)

(f)   Complete the table below which contains information about protocols used in clinical trials.

2

Protocol	Description
	Neither the experimenter nor the participant are aware of the treatment given to the participant
Placebo controlled	

7.   The graph below shows changes in the concentration of glucose and insulin in the blood of a woman cycling at a constant rate for two hours.

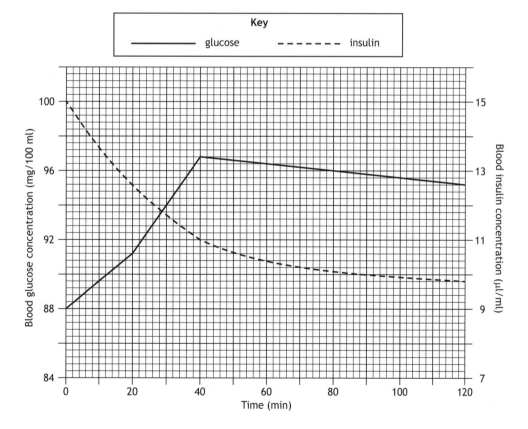

(a)   (i)   State the blood insulin level after 10 minutes cycling.   1

_____

(ii)   State the blood glucose concentration when the blood insulin was 11 µl per ml.   1

_____ mg per 100ml

MARKS | DO NOT WRITE IN THIS MARGIN

7. **(continued)**

(b) During strenuous exercise, adrenaline is released which inhibits the production of insulin.

Explain the importance of this to the cyclist.   2

_____

_____

(c) Name the substance into which excess glucose is converted for storage in the liver and muscles.   1

_____

(d) Describe the difference between type 1 and type 2 diabetes in terms of insulin production.   1

_____

_____

8. The diagram below shows how hormones from the pituitary gland affect the ovary.

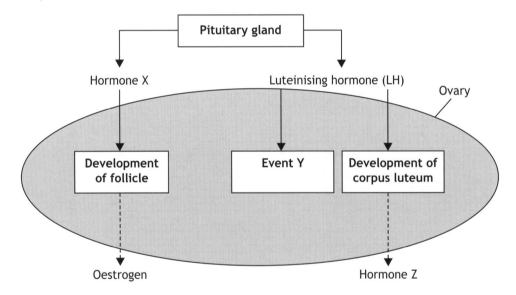

(a)   (i) Name hormones X and Z.   1

X _____

Z _____

(ii) Give the term used to describe Event Y.   1

_____

MARKS | DO NOT WRITE IN THIS MARGIN

8. **(a)** **(continued)**

(iii) Describe one effect of oestrogen on **the uterus**.   1

_____

_____

(b) Describe the effects of oral contraceptives on the pituitary gland.   1

_____

_____

9. The diagram below shows a section through an artery.

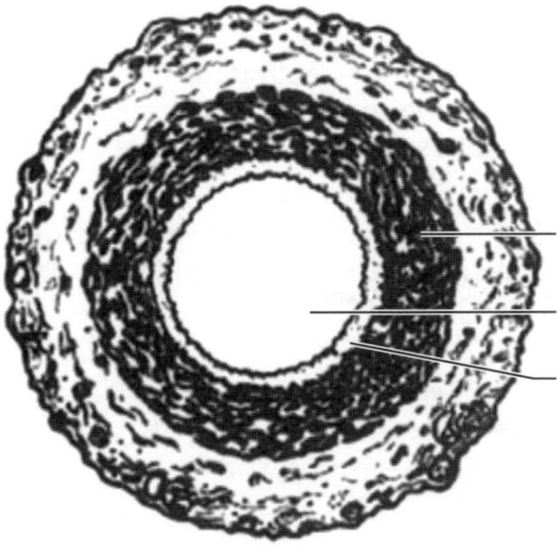

Layer with elastic fibres

P

Endothelium layer

(a)   **(i)** Name part P.   1

_____

(ii) Describe the effect of vasoconstriction on part P and how this would change blood flow through the artery.   1

Effect_____

Change in blood flow_____

MARKS | DO NOT WRITE IN THIS MARGIN

9.   **(continued)**

(b) Damage to the endothelium layer can lead to the formation of a thrombus.

Describe the formation of a thrombus at the site of endothelial damage.   **2**

_____

_____

_____

(c) Describe the role of the elastic fibres in the wall of an artery.   **1**

_____

_____

10. Receptors on the membranes of neurons are activated by natural neurotransmitters and by agonistic drugs which mimic neurotransmitter action. Activation of these receptors produces an electrical response by the neuron.

Graph 1 below shows the results of an investigation into the effects of the concentration of the agonistic drugs morphine and buprenorphine on the electrical response of neurons.

Graph 1

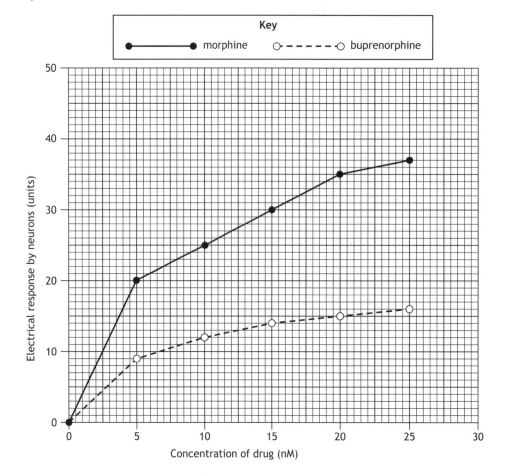

10. (continued)

Antagonistic drugs can block the effects of neurotransmitters and agonistic drugs.

Graph 2 below shows how neurons treated with a 1nM solution of morphine responded to increasing concentration of an experimental antagonistic drug.

Graph 2

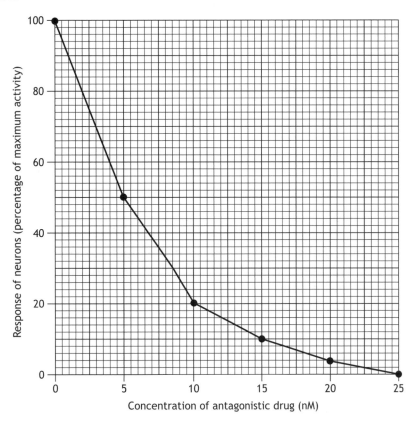

(a) Using information in **Graph 1**:

(i) Calculate the difference in response between the use of 15nM morphine and 15nM buprenorphine.   1

Space for calculation

_____ units

(ii) Calculate the percentage increase in response when the concentration of morphine was increased from 5 nM to 10 nM.   1

Space for calculation

_____ %

MARKS | DO NOT WRITE IN THIS MARGIN

10. (a) (continued)

(iii) **Using values from the graph**, describe the effect of increasing the concentration of buprenorphine on the electrical response by neurons.

1

_____

_____

(iv) Predict the electrical response of neurons if they were exposed to 30nM of morphine.

1

_____ units

(b) Using information in **Graphs 1 and 2**, calculate the electrical activity in the neurons which had been exposed to 1 nM morphine and 5 nM of the experimental antagonistic drug.

1

Space for calculation

_____ units

(c) Using information in **Graph 2**, give the concentration of the antagonistic drug needed to reduce the neuron response by 70%.

1

_____ nM

MARKS | DO NOT WRITE IN THIS MARGIN

11. The diagram below shows processes involved in memory.

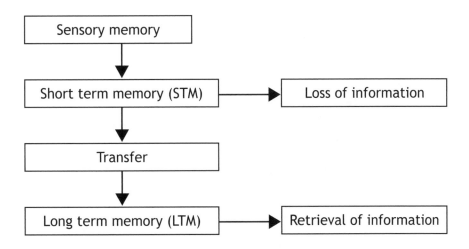

(a) Explain why some information can be displaced from the STM and lost as shown in the diagram.   **1**

_____

_____

(b) Name **two** methods for transferring information from the STM to the LTM.   **1**

1 _____

2 _____

(c) Retrieval of information can be aided by the use of contextual cues.

Explain what is meant by a contextual cue.   **1**

_____

_____

(d) Complete the table below to show the region(s) of the brain involved in the storage of the different types of memories.   **2**

Type of memory	Region of brain involved in storage
Procedural	
Semantic	
Spatial	

MARKS | DO NOT WRITE IN THIS MARGIN

12. The diagram below shows cells in a region of the skin which has been damaged by a sharp piece of wood.

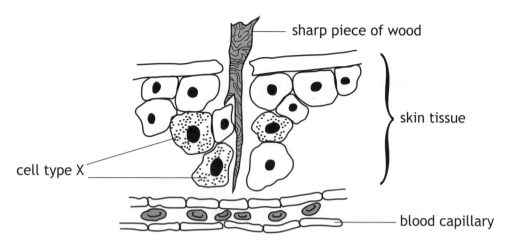

The flow chart below shows some of the events which result from the injury shown.

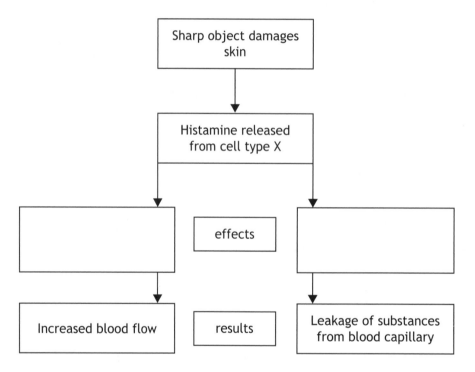

(a) Identify cell type X. 1

_____

(b) Complete the flow chart above to show the effects of histamine release. 2

MARKS | DO NOT WRITE IN THIS MARGIN

12.   (continued)

(c)   Name **one** substance which leaks from blood capillaries and describe how it protects against infection.

Substance _____   1

Description _____   1

_____

13.   The diagram below shows how a cell in the immune system responds to polio virus in a vaccine.

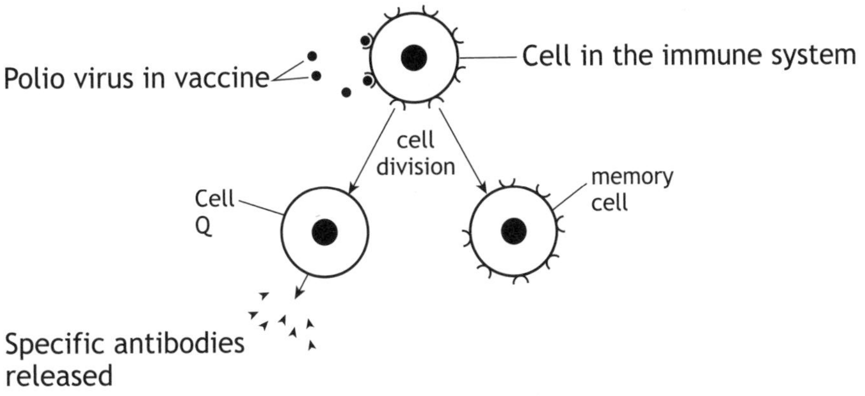

(a)   Name the substances present in vaccines which trigger an immune response.   1

_____

(b)   (i)   Name cell type Q.   1

_____

(ii)   Describe the specificity of the antibodies shown in the diagram.   1

_____

_____

(c)   Describe **one** difference which would be expected in the response of the immune system to a second exposure to the polio virus.   1

_____

_____

MARKS | DO NOT WRITE IN THIS MARGIN

14. Describe the general methods by which individuals and communities control infectious disease.

5

Space for answer

_____

_____

_____

_____

_____

_____

_____

_____

_____

_____

15. **Note that Question 15 contains a choice.**

Answer **either A or B** in the space below.

A   Describe the structure and replication of a molecule of DNA.   9

OR

B   Describe metabolism and the mode of action of enzymes in the control of metabolic pathways.   9

Space for answer

[END OF MODEL PAPER]

ADDITIONAL SPACE FOR ANSWERS AND ROUGH WORK

MARKS | DO NOT WRITE IN THIS MARGIN

ADDITIONAL SPACE FOR ANSWERS AND ROUGH WORK

Additional Graph for Question 6 (d)

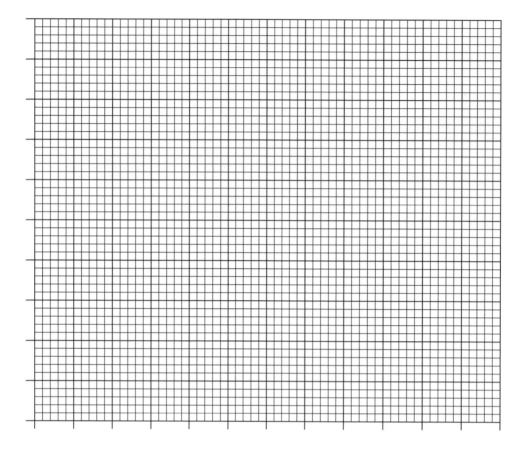

ADDITIONAL SPACE FOR ANSWERS AND ROUGH WORK

MARKS | DO NOT WRITE IN THIS MARGIN

ADDITIONAL SPACE FOR ANSWERS AND ROUGH WORK

HIGHER FOR CfE

2015

National
Qualifications
2015

X740/76/02

Human Biology
Section 1 — Questions

WEDNESDAY, 13 MAY
1:00 PM – 3:30 PM

Instructions for the completion of Section 1 are given on *Page two* of your question and answer booklet.

Record your answers on the answer grid on *Page three* of your question and answer booklet.

Before leaving the examination room you must give your question and answer booklet to the Invigilator; if you do not you may lose all the marks for this paper.

SECTION 1 — 20 marks

Attempt ALL questions

1. The diagram below shows an enzyme-catalysed reaction taking place in the presence of an inhibitor.

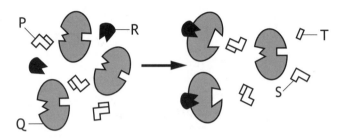

Which line in the table below identifies the molecules in the reaction?

	Inhibitor	Substrate	Product
A	P	R	S
B	Q	P	S
C	R	P	T
D	R	Q	T

2. A primary transcript is a strand of

    A   RNA comprising just exons

    B   DNA comprising just exons

    C   RNA comprising introns and exons

    D   DNA comprising introns and exons.

3. The diagram below can be used to identify amino acids coded for by mRNA codons.

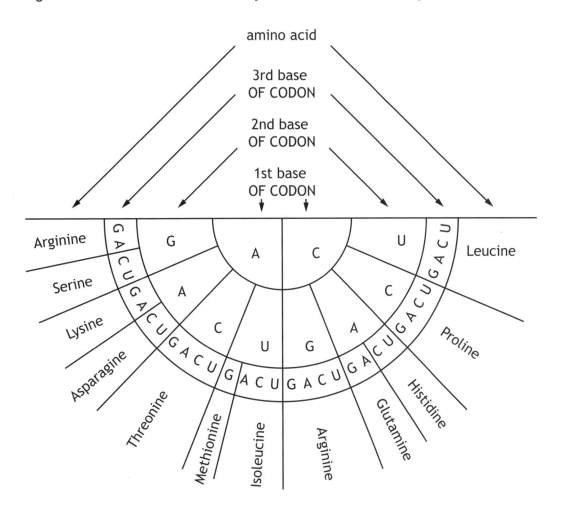

How many different amino acids are coded for by the following mRNA strand?

A U G C C A A C U C C U A G A C G A A U A

A   4

B   5

C   6

D   7

[Turn over

4. The following are descriptions of three single gene mutations.

    Description 1: exon-intron codons are created or destroyed

    Description 2: one amino acid codon is replaced with another

    Description 3: one amino acid codon is replaced with a stop codon

    Which line in the table below matches the descriptions with the correct gene mutation?

	Gene mutation		
	Missense	Nonsense	Splice site
A	1	2	3
B	1	3	2
C	2	1	3
D	2	3	1

5. DNA profiling may be used in criminal investigations.

    During this procedure DNA is cut into fragments by two different enzymes. Each enzyme cuts DNA at a specific point.

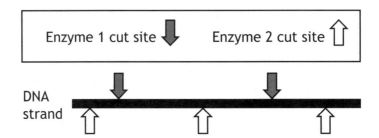

    Which line in the table below gives the correct number of DNA fragments produced from this DNA strand?

	Number of fragments produced using		
	enzyme 1 only	enzyme 2 only	enzymes 1 and 2
A	2	3	5
B	2	3	6
C	3	4	7
D	3	4	6

6. The graph below shows the changes to the concentrations of substrate and product during an enzyme-controlled reaction.

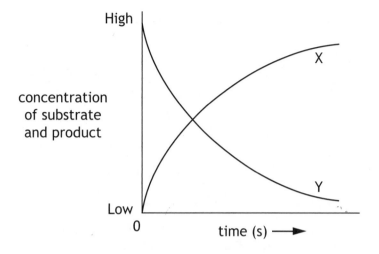

Which line in the table below identifies the substrate, product and the change in the rate of the reaction during the process?

	Substrate	Product	Rate of reaction
A	X	Y	increasing
B	X	Y	decreasing
C	Y	X	increasing
D	Y	X	decreasing

[Turn over

7. The graph below shows the rate of potassium uptake and glucose breakdown by muscle tissue in solutions of different oxygen concentrations.

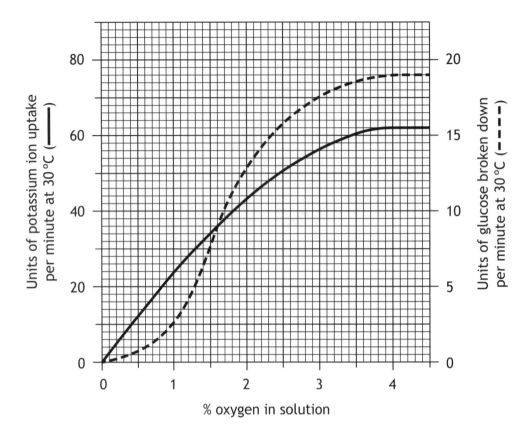

How much glucose is broken down per minute when the oxygen concentration is 1%?

A   2·5 units

B   6 units

C   10 units

D   24 units

8. A 40 g serving of a breakfast cereal contains 2 mg of iron. Only 25% of this iron is absorbed into the bloodstream.

If a pregnant woman requires a daily uptake of 6 mg of iron, how much cereal would she have to eat each day to meet this requirement?

A   60 g

B   120 g

C   240 g

D   480 g

9. The diagram below shows a section through part of the testes.

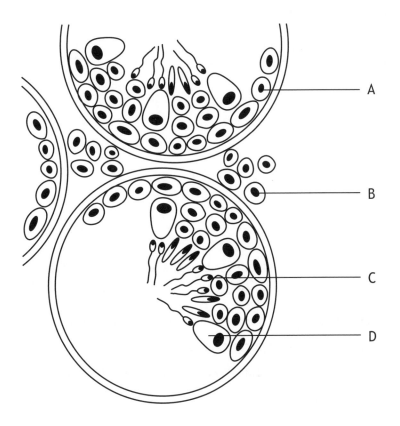

Which cells produce testosterone?

10. The table below shows some genotypes and phenotypes associated with forms of sickle-cell anaemia.

Genotype	Phenotype
AA	unaffected
AS	sickle-cell trait
SS	acute sickle-cell anaemia

A woman with sickle-cell trait and an unaffected man have a child together.

What are the chances that their child will have acute sickle-cell anaemia?

A   None

B   1 in 1

C   1 in 2

D   1 in 4

[Turn over

11. The events leading to formation of a blood clot are listed below.

    1.   Clotting factors are released.
    2.   An insoluble meshwork forms.
    3.   Fibrinogen is converted to fibrin.
    4.   Prothrombin is converted to thrombin.

The correct sequence of these events is

A   4, 2, 3, 1

B   1, 4, 3, 2

C   1, 3, 4, 2

D   4, 3, 1, 2

12. Which of the following statements describes the role of lipoprotein in the transport and elimination of excess cholesterol?

A   Low density lipoprotein transports excess cholesterol from the liver to the body cells.

B   Low density lipoprotein transports excess cholesterol from the body cells to the liver.

C   High density lipoprotein transports excess cholesterol from the liver to the body cells.

D   High density lipoprotein transports excess cholesterol from the body cells to the liver.

13. Which of the following describes typical features of Type 1 diabetes?

	Feature of Type 1 diabetes	
A	occurs in childhood	cells unable to produce insulin
B	develops later in life	cells unable to produce insulin
C	occurs in childhood	cells less sensitive to insulin
D	develops later in life	cells less sensitive to insulin

14. The following are types of neural pathways.

    1. Diverging
    2. Converging
    3. Reverberating

    Which of these pathways involve nerve impulses being sent back through a circuit of neurons?

    A   3 only

    B   1 and 2 only

    C   1 and 3 only

    D   1, 2 and 3

15. After drinking, alcohol is removed from the blood at a constant rate.

    The table below shows the average time it takes to remove different alcohol concentrations from the blood.

Blood alcohol concentration (mg/100 cm^3)	Removal time (hours)
16	1·0
50	3·125
80	5·0
100	6·25
160	10·0
200	12·5

    The legal maximum blood alcohol concentration for driving in some regions of the UK is 80 mg/100 cm^3.

    Predict how long it would take before a person with a blood alcohol concentration of 240 mg/100 cm^3 would legally be able to drive in these regions.

    A   5 hours

    B   10 hours

    C   15 hours

    D   20 hours

[Turn over

16. A number of students were trained to carry out a complex task. Some competed with one another, others worked in isolation.

The graph below shows the number of errors recorded in the training process.

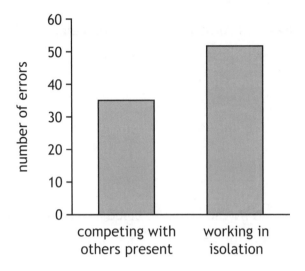

Which process is likely to have caused the difference in the results?

A   Deindividuation

B   Social facilitation

C   Shaping

D   Internalisation

17. The pathogen for the disease tuberculosis (TB) evades the specific immune response by

A   surviving within phagocytes

B   attacking lymphocytes

C   attacking phagocytes

D   antigenic variation.

18. The graph below shows the average growth rate of body organs in males.

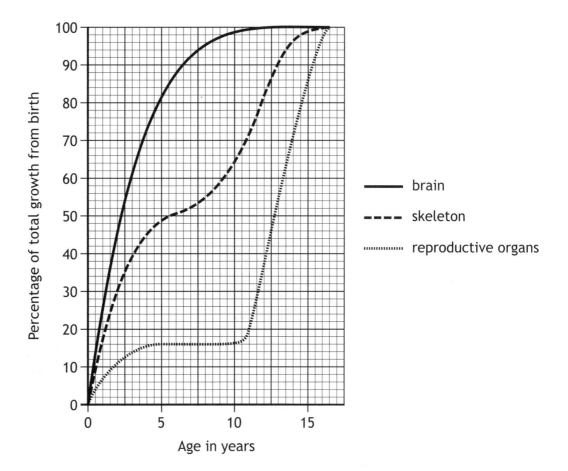

What is the ratio of total growth of brain to skeleton in an 8 year old child?

A   11 : 3

B   3 : 11

C   19 : 11

D   11 : 19

19. Failure in regulation of the immune system leading to an autoimmune disease is caused by a

A   B lymphocyte immune response to self antigens.

B   T lymphocyte immune response to self antigens.

C   B lymphocyte immune response to foreign antigens.

D   T lymphocyte immune response to foreign antigens.

[Turn over for Question 20 on *Page twelve*

20. Blood tests to measure the number of white blood cells (leucocytes) are often used to indicate infection and/or illness.

Leucopenia, due to starvation or malnutrition, is indicated by white blood cell numbers dropping below 4×10^9/litre.

Leucocytosis, due to fever or tissue damage, is indicated by white blood cell numbers temporarily increasing to 11×10^9/litre.

Leukaemia, due to DNA damage and cell division, is indicated by white blood cell numbers permanently increasing.

The following graphs show the white blood cell count of four patients over 20 weeks.

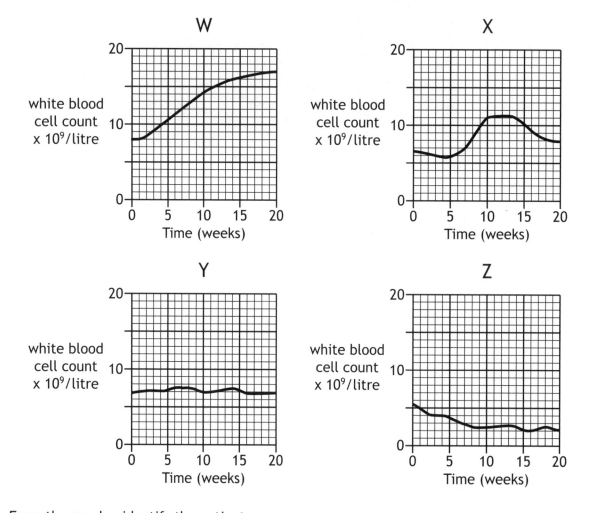

From the graphs, identify the patients.

	Leukaemia	Leucocytosis	Leucopenia
A	Y	X	Z
B	Z	W	Y
C	W	X	Z
D	W	Y	X

**[END OF SECTION 1. NOW ATTEMPT THE QUESTIONS IN SECTION 2
OF YOUR QUESTION AND ANSWER BOOKLET.]**

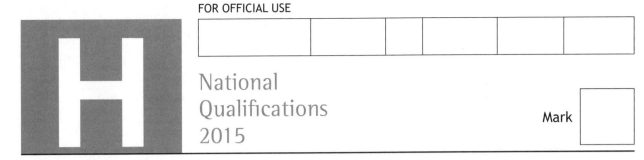

H

National Qualifications 2015

Mark

X740/76/01

Human Biology
Section 1 — Answer Grid and Section 2

WEDNESDAY, 13 MAY

1:00 PM – 3:30 PM

Fill in these boxes and read what is printed below.

Full name of centre

Town

Forename(s)

Surname

Number of seat

Date of birth

Day   Month   Year

Scottish candidate number

Total marks — 100

SECTION 1 — 20 marks

Attempt ALL questions.

Instructions for completion of Section 1 are given on *Page two*.

SECTION 2 — 80 marks

Attempt ALL questions.

Write your answers clearly in the spaces provided in this booklet. Additional space for answers and rough work is provided at the end of this booklet. If you use this space you must clearly identify the question number you are attempting. Any rough work must be written in this booklet. You should score through your rough work when you have written your final copy.

Use **blue** or **black** ink.

Before leaving the examination room you must give this booklet to the Invigilator; if you do not, you may lose all the marks for this paper.

SECTION 1— 20 marks

The questions for Section 1 are contained in the question paper X740/76/02.
Read these and record your answers on the answer grid on *Page three* opposite.
Use **blue** or **black** ink. Do NOT use gel pens or pencil.

1. The answer to each question is **either** A, B, C or D. Decide what your answer is, then fill in the appropriate bubble (see sample question below).

2. There is **only one correct** answer to each question.

3. Any rough working should be done on the additional space for answers and rough work at the end of this booklet.

Sample Question

The digestive enzyme pepsin is most active in the

    A   mouth

    B   stomach

    C   duodenum

    D   pancreas.

The correct answer is **B**—stomach. The answer **B** bubble has been clearly filled in (see below).

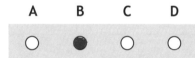

Changing an answer

If you decide to change your answer, cancel your first answer by putting a cross through it (see below) and fill in the answer you want. The answer below has been changed to **D**.

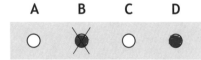

If you then decide to change back to an answer you have already scored out, put a tick (✓) to the **right** of the answer you want, as shown below:

SECTION 1 — Answer Grid

	A	B	C	D
1	○	○	○	○
2	○	○	○	○
3	○	○	○	○
4	○	○	○	○
5	○	○	○	○
6	○	○	○	○
7	○	○	○	○
8	○	○	○	○
9	○	○	○	○
10	○	○	○	○
11	○	○	○	○
12	○	○	○	○
13	○	○	○	○
14	○	○	○	○
15	○	○	○	○
16	○	○	○	○
17	○	○	○	○
18	○	○	○	○
19	○	○	○	○
20	○	○	○	○

[BLANK PAGE]

DO NOT WRITE ON THIS PAGE

[Turn over for Section 2 on *Page six*

DO NOT WRITE ON THIS PAGE

MARKS | DO NOT WRITE IN THIS MARGIN

SECTION 2 — 80 marks

Attempt ALL questions

Note that Question 14 contains a choice

1. The diagram below represents an embryo in the early stages of development and identifies the inner cell mass which is made up of stem cells.

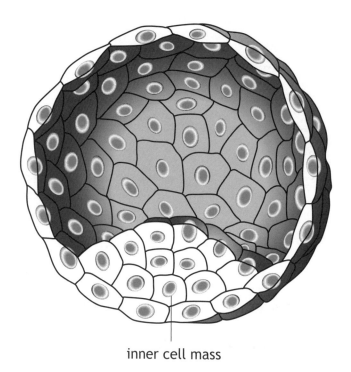

inner cell mass

(a) State one feature of stem cells.

1

_____

_____

(b) Stem cells are also found in tissues throughout the adult body.

Explain how the function of tissue stem cells differs from that of the stem cells found in the inner cell mass of an embryo.

1

_____

_____

MARKS | DO NOT WRITE IN THIS MARGIN

1. **(continued)**

(c) Stem cells have uses in both therapy and research.

(i) It has been proposed that tissue cells could be used to repair severely damaged muscle tissue.

Suggest how this might be done.   1

_____

_____

_____

(ii) State how stem cells can be used as model cells in medical research.   1

_____

_____

[Turn over

MARKS | DO NOT WRITE IN THIS MARGIN

2. Glycogen storage disease is an inherited condition in which the enzyme glycogen synthase does not function.

This enzyme normally catalyses one step in the conversion of glucose to glycogen, for storage, as shown in the diagram below.

enzyme 1   enzyme 2   glycogen synthase

glucose ————→ compound A ————→ compound B ————→ glycogen

(a) State the term which describes a metabolic pathway in which simple molecules are built up into complex molecules.   **1**

_____

(b) (i) Describe how the genetic code for glycogen synthase might be altered in an individual with the disease.   **1**

_____

_____

(ii) Explain why this altered genetic code fails to produce glycogen synthase.   **1**

_____

_____

(c) Suggest why individuals with glycogen storage disease might develop abnormally low blood glucose levels during exercise.   **1**

_____

_____

_____

(d) One form of glycogen storage disease is caused by a gene which is recessive and sex-linked.

Describe a pattern of inheritance, shown by a family history, which would indicate that the condition is   **2**

recessive _____

_____

sex-linked _____

_____

MARKS | DO NOT WRITE IN THIS MARGIN

3. Most skin cancers are caused by overexposure to ultraviolet (UV) radiation from the sun or sunbeds. UV radiation damages the DNA in skin cells. Cells normally repair this damage but those which cannot may become cancerous.

A student designed an investigation which used UV-sensitive yeast cells to show the damaging effect of UV radiation. These yeast cells cannot repair DNA damage and die after exposure to UV radiation.

A suspension of UV-sensitive yeast cells was added to dishes which contained a gel that had all the nutrients the yeast needed to grow. The dishes were then exposed to UV radiation for different lengths of time. After exposure, the dishes were placed in an incubator and each of the surviving yeast cells left to grow into a colony on the gel. The number of these colonies was then counted.

The diagram below illustrates this procedure.

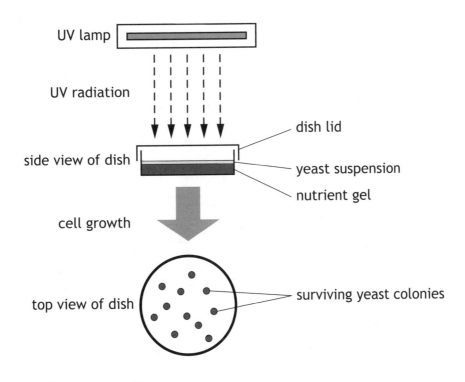

(a) List **two** variables which should be kept constant during this investigation.

2

1 _____

2 _____

[Turn over

MARKS | DO NOT WRITE IN THIS MARGIN

3. (continued)

(b) The results of the investigation are shown in **Table 1** below.

Table 1 — Yeast growth after exposure to UV radiation

Length of time of exposure (minutes)	Number of yeast colonies growing
10	58
20	32
30	15
40	4
50	1
60	0

  (i)   Plot a line graph to illustrate the results of the investigation.   2

(Additional graph paper, if required can be found on *Page thirty-one*)

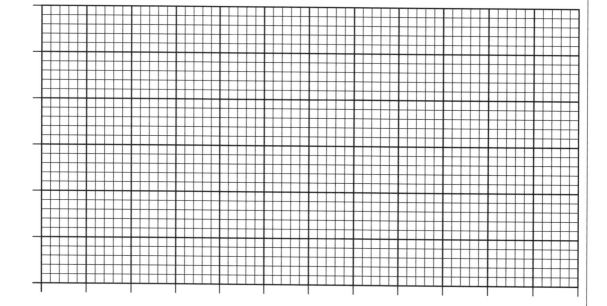

  (ii)   State a conclusion that can be drawn from these results.   1

_____

_____

  (iii)   State how the reliability of the results in this investigation could be improved.   1

_____

_____

3. (continued)

(c) Sunscreens work by blocking UV radiation, preventing it from entering skin cells and causing damage to the DNA, which results in sunburn.

Sunscreens are labelled with a Sun Protection Factor (SPF).

When a sunscreen of SPF 15 is applied to the skin, it will take 15 times longer to burn compared to having no sunscreen applied.

The student carried out a second investigation using UV-sensitive yeast.

The dishes were prepared as before but this time the lids of the dishes were coated with sunscreen of different SPFs. The dishes were then exposed to UV radiation for 30 minutes. After exposure, the dishes were placed in an incubator and the surviving yeast cells left to grow into colonies. The results are shown in **Table 2** below.

Table 2 — Yeast growth after the use of sunscreen protection

Sunscreen used to coat lid (SPF)	Number of yeast colonies growing
6	20
15	72
35	74
50	75

(i) Use the information from **Tables 1 and 2** to calculate the percentage increase in yeast cell survival when a sunscreen of SPF 50 is used to coat the lid.   1

Space for calculation

_____ %

(ii) Official health advice recommends that people should use a sunscreen of SPF 15 when sunbathing for 30 minutes.

State how the results of this investigation support this recommendation.   1

_____

_____

_____

(iii) If skin starts to burn after 10 minutes in strong sunlight, calculate for how long a sunscreen of SPF 35 would protect the skin.   1

Space for calculation

_____

MARKS | DO NOT WRITE IN THIS MARGIN

4. The diagram below represents **three** chemical reactions in the energy investment phase of glycolysis.

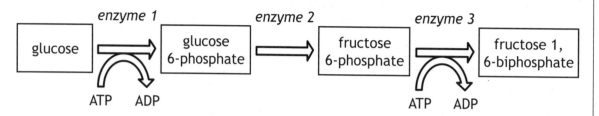

(a) Identify the information, shown **in the diagram**, which confirms that this is the energy investment phase of glycolysis.

1

_____

_____

(b) Enzyme 1 is activated by the binding of magnesium ions.

Suggest how the binding of these ions leads to an increase in enzyme activity.

1

_____

_____

(c) Choose an enzyme shown **in the diagram** which is catalysing a phosphorylation reaction.

Circle **one** enzyme —   Enzyme 1   Enzyme 2   Enzyme 3

Explain what is meant by phosphorylation.

1

_____

_____

(d) The conversion of glucose 6-phosphate to fructose 6-phosphate is a reversible reaction.

Describe the circumstances under which this reaction would go in the opposite direction to that shown in the diagram.

1

_____

_____

(e) Following the energy investment phase, glycolysis enters the energy pay off stage, during which ATP is produced.

Enzyme 3 is phosphofructokinase which is inhibited by a build-up of ATP.

Explain how this feedback mechanism conserves the cell's resources.

1

_____

_____

MARKS | DO NOT WRITE IN THIS MARGIN

5. Muscle cells utilise a variety of energy systems during strenuous activity.

(a) Creatine phosphate is found in muscle cells.

(i) Describe how creatine phosphate supports strenuous muscle activity.

2

_____

_____

_____

_____

(ii) Explain why this support is not provided to strenuous activities beyond the first 10 seconds.

1

_____

_____

(b) Name the substance which builds up in muscle cells as they become fatigued.

1

_____

(c) Choose a sporting activity and decide whether slow twitch or fast twitch muscle fibres would be best suited for the activity.

Sporting Activity _____

Slow twitch ☐   Fast twitch ☐

Give reasons to justify your choice of muscle fibre.

3

_____

_____

_____

_____

_____

_____

_____

[Turn over

MARKS | DO NOT WRITE IN THIS MARGIN

6. Chorionic villus sampling (CVS) is a technique which can be used during antenatal screening. The cells obtained from CVS are used to prepare a karyotype.

(a) The diagram below shows the uterus of a pregnant woman with a section of the placenta enlarged.

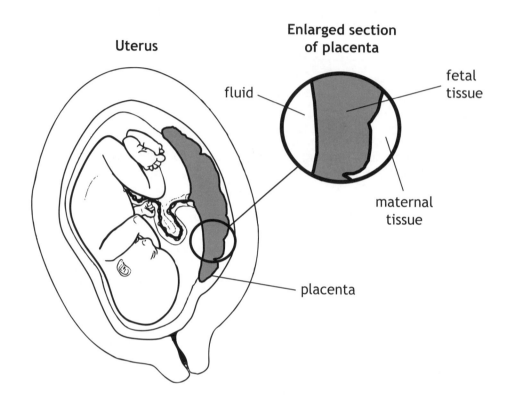

(i)   Place a cross (X) on the diagram of the **enlarged section of placenta** to indicate the area from which cells are removed during CVS.

1

(ii) Describe the process by which a karyotype is produced from cells removed during CVS.

2

_____

_____

_____

_____

(iii) Suggest an advantage of using CVS rather than amniocentesis during antenatal screening.

1

_____

_____

MARKS | DO NOT WRITE IN THIS MARGIN

6. **(continued)**

(b) Name the type of antenatal screening tests which are routinely carried out to monitor the concentration of certain substances, such as protein, in a pregnant woman's blood.

1

_____

[Turn over

MARKS | DO NOT WRITE IN THIS MARGIN

7. The graph below contains information about the body mass index (BMI) of Scottish children in 2009.

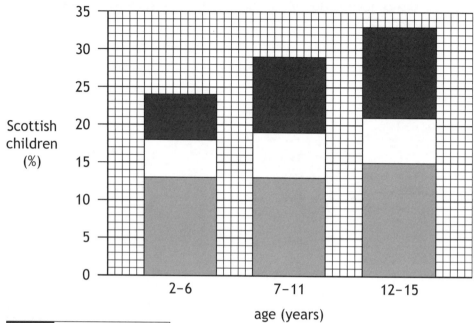

Scottish children (%)

age (years)

	MORBIDLY OBESE BMI above 35
	OBESE BMI 30 to 34·9
	OVERWEIGHT BMI 25 to 29·9

(a) State the percentage of children aged 12 to 15 who had a BMI of more than 30 in 2009.

Space for calculation

1

_____ %

(b) Suggest reasons why the percentage of obese children increased between the ages of 2 and 15.

1

_____

_____

MARKS | DO NOT WRITE IN THIS MARGIN

7. (continued)

(c) Explain how BMI is calculated.   **1**

_____

_____

(d) Suggest how children could be encouraged to maintain a healthy BMI by
use of the following processes.   **2**

Identification _____

_____

Internalisation _____

_____

[Turn over

8. The heart rate and stroke volume of a 40 year old cyclist were monitored as he used an exercise bike.

    The cyclist was told to pedal at a constant rate as his work level was gradually raised by increasing the resistance to pedalling.

    The graph below shows the changes that occurred in the cyclist's heart rate and stroke volume at seven different work levels.

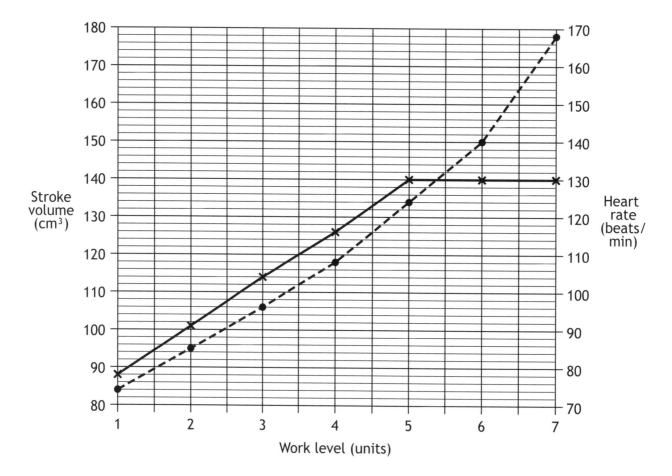

KEY

✕——————✕ stroke volume - volume of blood pumped out per heartbeat

●– – – –● heart rate - beats of heart per minute

MARKS | DO NOT WRITE IN THIS MARGIN

8. **(continued)**

(a) Use **data from the graph** to describe the changes that occurred in the cyclist's stroke volume when the work level increased from 1 to 7 units. **2**

_____

_____

_____

_____

(b) State what the cyclist's heart rate was when his stroke volume was 120 cm³. **1**

Space for calculation

_____ beats/min

(c) Cardiac output is the volume of blood leaving the heart in one minute. It is calculated using the formula shown below.

cardiac output = heart rate × stroke volume

Calculate the cyclist's cardiac output when his work level was 6 units. **1**

Space for calculation

_____ cm³/min

[Turn over

8. **(continued)**

(d) The table below shows the recommended minimum heart rates that cyclists of different ages should maintain in order to either metabolise fat or improve their fitness.

Age	Minimum heart rate for metabolising fat (beats/min)	Minimum heart rate for improving fitness (beats/min)
10	136	168
20	130	160
30	123	152
40	116	144
50	110	136
60	104	128

(i) Use information from the **table** and the **graph** to determine the work level that the cyclist should maintain in order to metabolise fat.

1

_____ units

(ii) Use information from the **table** to predict the minimum heart rate for improving the fitness of a 70 year old.

1

_____

(iii) As an individual gets older, their minimum heart rate for improving fitness decreases.

Use the information from the **table** to calculate the percentage decrease that occurs between the ages of 10 and 60 years.

1

Space for calculation

_____ %

MARKS DO NOT WRITE IN THIS MARGIN

9. The diagram below shows some nerve cells involved in a neural reward pathway.

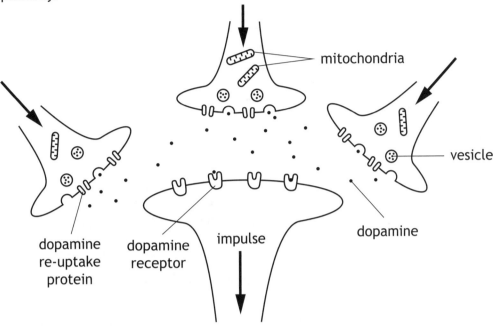

(a) Using information from the diagram, explain what is meant by the term "summation".　　1

_____

_____

(b) Suggest a function for the mitochondria shown in the diagram.　　1

_____

_____

(c) Cocaine is a recreational drug that has an effect at this synapse.

Cocaine binds to the dopamine re-uptake proteins. As a result, the reward pathway is stimulated for longer.

Suggest how cocaine produces this effect.　　2

_____

_____

_____

_____

MARKS | DO NOT WRITE IN THIS MARGIN

10. A biology student produced the following diagram as a memory aid to help her learn about transport in plants.

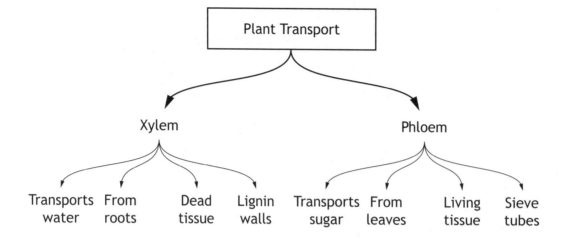

(a) In producing this diagram the student used various methods to learn the information.

Other than rehearsal, name **two** methods that she used and describe how they helped her transfer the information into her long-term memory.

2

1   Method _____

Description _____

_____

2   Method _____

Description _____

_____

(b) Any information which is not transferred into long-term memory is displaced. Explain why displacement occurs.

1

_____

_____

(c) The student is storing a record of facts as she learns this information. State the part of the brain in which such memories are stored.

1

_____

MARKS | DO NOT WRITE IN THIS MARGIN

11. Various types of white blood cell are involved in the non-specific immune response.

(a) Describe the role of each of the following cells in the non-specific defence of the body.

    (i) Mast cells _____   **2**

_____

_____

_____

    (ii) Natural killer (NK) cells _____   **1**

_____

_____

_____

(b) Explain how the presence of phagocytes is important in the activation of T lymphocytes.   **2**

_____

_____

_____

_____

[Turn over

MARKS | DO NOT WRITE IN THIS MARGIN

12. HIV is a virus which invades the cells of the immune system.

People infected with HIV may not show symptoms for many years.

AIDS is the condition which may develop from HIV infection, resulting in death.

The graph below shows the number of people in the world infected with HIV, from 1990 to 2010. It also shows the number of people who died from AIDS during this period.

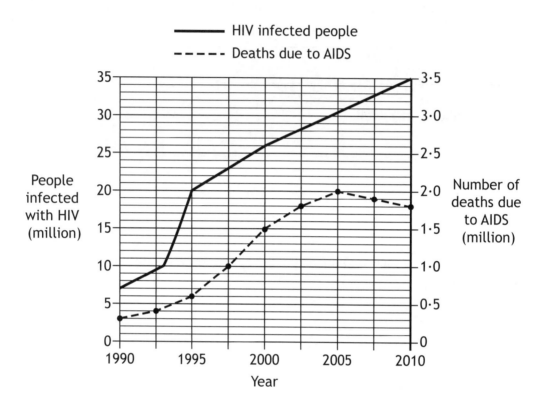

(a) State how many people were infected with HIV in the year 2000. 1

_____

(b) State how many people died from AIDS when 20 million people in the world were infected with HIV. 1

_____

(c) Calculate the percentage of HIV-infected people who died from AIDS in 2010. 1

Space for calculation

_____ %

MARKS | DO NOT WRITE IN THIS MARGIN

12. **(continued)**

(d) Describe the evidence from the graph which suggests that the rate of people becoming infected with HIV was greatest between 1993 and 1995.

1

_____

_____

[Turn over

MARKS | DO NOT WRITE IN THIS MARGIN

13. A scientist investigated the effectiveness of four different types of influenza vaccine. A total of 2000 volunteers from a Scottish community were divided into four groups.

Each group was injected with a different vaccine.

The number who developed influenza during the following years was recorded.

The results are shown in the table below.

Type of influenza vaccine	Developed influenza	Did not develop influenza	Total
P	35	495	530
Q	25	455	480
R	24	496	520
S	17		

(a) (i) Suggest **one** way in which the scientist could minimise variation between the four groups of volunteers.

1

(ii) **Complete the table** for the volunteers who received type S vaccine.

1

(iii) State which of the vaccines P, Q or R was most effective in this investigation.

1

(b) Explain why vaccines usually contain an adjuvant.

1

(c) In 1918 fifty million people died in a global outbreak of influenza.

State the term used to describe such an outbreak.

1

MARKS

DO NOT WRITE IN THIS MARGIN

14. Answer **either** A **or** B in the space below.

Labelled diagrams may be used where appropriate.

A   Describe hormonal control of the menstrual cycle under the following headings:

    (i)   events leading to ovulation;   **6**

    (ii)   events following ovulation.   **4**

OR

B   Describe the cardiac cycle under the following headings:

    (i)   the conducting system of the heart;   **5**

    (ii)   nervous control of the cardiac cycle.   **5**

[Turn over

ADDITIONAL SPACE FOR ANSWER TO QUESTION 14

MARKS | DO NOT WRITE IN THIS MARGIN

[END OF QUESTION PAPER]

MARKS | DO NOT WRITE IN THIS MARGIN

ADDITIONAL SPACE FOR ANSWERS AND ROUGH WORK

MARKS | DO NOT WRITE IN THIS MARGIN

ADDITIONAL SPACE FOR ANSWERS AND ROUGH WORK

ADDITIONAL GRAPH PAPER FOR QUESTION 3 (b) (i)

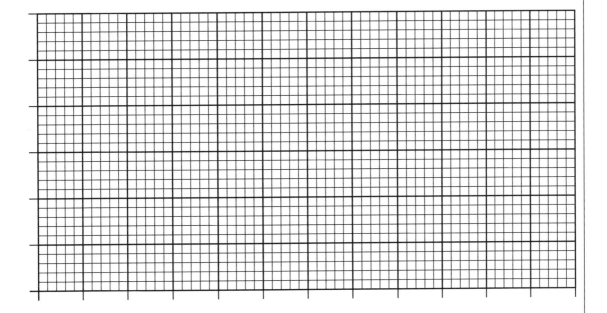

[BLANK PAGE]

DO NOT WRITE ON THIS PAGE

HIGHER FOR CfE | ANSWER SECTION

SQA AND HODDER GIBSON HIGHER FOR CfE HUMAN BIOLOGY 2015

Section 1

Question	Answer	Mark
1.	A	1
2.	C	1
3.	B	1
4.	D	1
5.	A	1
6.	C	1
7.	B	1
8.	D	1
9.	B	1
10.	A	1
11.	D	1
12.	C	1
13.	C	1
14.	B	1
15.	D	1
16.	A	1
17.	C	1
18.	D	1
19.	B	1
20.	B	1

Section 2

Question			Expected Answer(s)	Max mark
1.	(a)		Process – Differentiation. Explanation – only the genes characteristic for that cell are expressed	2
	(b)	(i)	Meiosis.	1
		(ii)	Mutations in germline cells can be passed to offspring (while mutations in somatic cells cannot)	1
	(c)		It is safer than using the drug directly on humans/trial subjects OR Is it right to use embryos to extract stem cells? OR Is it right to deprive sufferers of a potential treatment? OR Is it right to use stem cells rather than animals?	1
2.	(a)		RNA polymerase	1
	(b)		Translation **and** ribosome	1

Question			Expected Answer(s)	Max mark
	(c)	(i)	Only one gene is transcribed/forms mRNA OR The primary mRNA only codes for one protein	1
		(ii)	Introns/non-coding regions of genes are removed (in RNA splicing) OR The mature mRNA transcript only contains exons/coding regions of genes	1
3.	(a)		Correct scales and labels on axes Points correctly plotted and line drawn	2
	(b)	(i)	volume of urea solution OR volume of urease solution OR concentration of urease solution OR volume/length of agar/diameter of test tube OR volume/concentration of indicator in agar	1
		(ii)	Temperature of the tube contents/of the test tubes	1
	(c)		The experiment was repeated at each urea concentration (and an average calculated)	1
	(d)		To allow time for the ammonia to (fully) diffuse/spread through the agar/jelly	1
	(e)		As the urea concentration increased more ammonia was produced OR As the urea concentration decreased less ammonia was produced	1
	(f)		48	1
	(g)	(i)	Thiourea blocked the active site on the urease/enzyme	1
		(ii)	Not all active sites were blocked OR some active sites were still available	1
4.	(a)		*Energy investment* – ATP molecules are broken down/used up (to provide energy) OR Phosphorylation/addition of phosphate to glucose/intermediates occur. *Energy pay-off* – ATP molecules are produced	2

Question			Expected Answer(s)	Max mark
	(b)		Acetyl (group)/acetyl coenzyme A/ acetyl CoA produced when oxygen is present/in aerobic conditions **OR** Lactic acid produced when oxygen is absent/insufficient/in anaerobic conditions	2
	(c)		Athlete — Sprinter Reason — creatine (phosphate) releases energy at a fast rate/for a short period of time/runs out quickly.	1
5.	(a)		SS	1
	(b)		50	1
	(c)	(i)	It alters the (DNA) <u>nucleotide sequence</u> **OR** <u>replaces one nucleotide</u> with another	1
		(ii)	An incorrect <u>amino acid</u> is placed in the protein/polypeptide chain/haemoglobin **OR** One <u>amino acid</u> is replaced by another in the protein/polypeptide chain/ haemoglobin **OR** The <u>amino acid</u> sequence is shortened (due to a stop codon)	1
	(d)		Pre-implantation Genetic Diagnosis/ PGD/pre-implantation genetic screening	1
	(e)		This drug could switch on the gene for fetal haemoglobin (in the child so haemoglobin is produced) **OR** This drug could stop the gene being switched off (in the child)	1
6.	(a)		It can contract/vasoconstrict to reduce blood flow to some areas **OR** It can relax/vasodilate to increase blood flow to some areas	1
	(b)		1. <u>Endothelium</u> is damaged 2. <u>Clotting factors</u> are released 3. <u>Prothrombin</u> (enzyme) is converted/ activated/changed into thrombin 4. <u>Fibrinogen</u> is converted into fibrin (by thrombin) 5. Fibrin/threads form a <u>meshwork</u> (that seals the wound) 6. The clot/thrombus formed may break loose, forming an <u>embolus</u> 7. A clot/thrombus may lead to a heart attack/stroke	5
7.	(a)	(i)	98 <u>beats/minute</u>	1
		(ii)	Stroke volume <u>increased</u> as oxygen uptake increased, <u>until 2 litres/min</u>, after which it <u>remained constant</u>.	1
		(iii)	150	1
	(b)		18·72	1

Question			Expected Answer(s)	Max mark
	(c)	(i)	The first figure is systolic blood pressure/when blood is surging through the arteries/when the artery wall is stretched <u>and</u> the second figure is diastolic blood pressure/when blood is not surging through the arteries/when the artery wall has recoiled	1
		(ii)	High blood pressure forces more fluid out of the <u>capillaries</u> <u>Lymph vessels</u> cannot reabsorb all the excess tissue fluid	2
8.	(a)	(i)	*A* — Diabetic because blood glucose concentration increases faster/to a higher level/for a longer time **OR** because blood glucose concentration does not return to normal (after 150 minutes) *B* — Non-diabetic because blood glucose increases slower/to a lower level/for a shorter time **OR** because blood glucose concentration returns to normal (after 60 minutes)	1
		(ii)	Blood glucose concentration increases for 60 minutes **and** then decreases At least one blood glucose concentration given with units eg Start = 4·8 m mol/litre 60 minutes = 11·2 m mol/litre 150 minutes = 7·6 m mol/litre	2
	(b)		Type 1 — Insulin is not produced <u>so</u> blood glucose concentration cannot be controlled Type 2 — Insulin is produced <u>but</u> cells are less sensitive to insulin/have fewer insulin receptors/have developed insulin resistance	2
9.	(a)	(i)	1. As age increases, the frequency/ number of cases of obesity increases 2. The frequency/number of cases is higher in 2012 (compared to 2003)	2
		(ii)	1·536 million/1 536 000	1
	(b)		Reduce their intake of fats/sugars/ carbohydrates **OR** exercise more/become more active	1
10.	(a)		85·5	1

Question		Expected Answer(s)	Max mark
	(b)	1. Each group has a similar gender balance 2. Each group completed the same jigsaw puzzle 3. Each group contained children with similar (physical/mental) abilities 4. The investigation was carried out in the same environmental conditions/same room/same temperature/same time of day/no distractions were present	2
	(c)	As children get older they <u>learn</u> faster (how to complete puzzles)	1
	(d) (i)	By the fifth attempt the children had learned/memorised where the pieces went (as a result of experience)	1
	(ii)	Some children had become bored with/lost interest in the puzzle (by the fifth attempt/through lack of reinforcement)	1
	(e)	Repeat the investigation in front of an audience/as a competition	1
11. (a) (i)		1955 or 1956	1
	(ii)	Decrease in vaccination rate/lack of vaccines available OR mass immigration OR mutation of the whooping cough bacteria OR adverse publicity about the vaccine	1
	(b)	A large percentage of the population have been immunised This means that there is a very low chance that non-immune individuals will come into contact with infected individuals	2
12. (a) (i)		Shorter life span/lower survival rate, so no time to develop heart disease	1
	(ii)	Better medical care/more doctors/more hospitals/more drugs OR more use of insecticides/vector control OR clean water/sewage treatment	1
	(b) (i)	20%	1
	(ii)	300 000	1
13. (a)		Inhaled air/droplet infection.	1
	(b) (i)	1986–1991	1
	(ii)	Increased vaccination OR more effective antibiotic treatment	1
	(iii)	Cases of pulmonary TB decreased between 1991 and 2006 <u>while</u> cases of non-pulmonary TB increased between 1991 and 2006	1
	(iv)	11 : 5	1

Question		Expected Answer(s)	Max mark
	(c)	HIV attacks <u>lymphocytes</u> reducing the ability of the immune system to respond to the bacterial infection	1
14. A		1. ANS works automatically/without conscious control 2. Impulses originate in the <u>medulla</u> (region of the brain) 3. It is made up of the sympathetic <u>and</u> parasympathetic systems 4. These two systems are <u>antagonistic</u> in action 5. The sympathetic system prepares the body for fight or flight 6. The parasympathetic system prepares the body for rest and digest 7. Correct description of the effect of the ANS in controlling heart rate 8. Correct description of the effect of the ANS in controlling breathing rate 9. Correct description of the effect of the ANS in controlling peristalsis 10. Correct description of the effect of the ANS in controlling intestinal secretions	7
	B	1. Neurotransmitters relay messages from nerve to nerve/muscle 2. Gap between them is called the <u>synaptic cleft</u> 3. Neurotransmitters are stored in <u>vesicles</u> 4. Arrival of an impulse causes vesicles to fuse with membrane <u>and</u> release neurotransmitter 5. Neurotransmitters <u>diffuse</u> across the cleft 6. Neurotransmitters bind to <u>receptors</u> 7. Receptors determine whether the signal is excitory or inhibitory 8. Neurotransmitters are removed by enzymes/re-uptake 9. Removal prevents continuous stimulation of post-synaptic neurones 10. Summation of weak stimuli can release enough neurotransmitter to fire an impulse	7

HIGHER FOR CfE HUMAN BIOLOGY MODEL PAPER 1

Section 1

Question	Answer	Mark
1.	C	1
2.	D	1
3.	B	1
4.	A	1
5.	B	1
6.	B	1
7.	A	1
8.	A	1
9.	B	1
10.	D	1
11.	C	1
12.	C	1
13.	C	1
14.	A	1
15.	B	1
16.	D	1
17.	C	1
18.	D	1
19.	B	1
20.	D	1

Section 2

Question			Expected Answer(s)	Max mark
1.	(a)		Differentiation	1
	(b)		Tissue stem cells give rise to a more limited range of cell type OR they divide to replace only cells of the type found in that particular tissue	1
	(c)		(Cancer cells) divide excessively/by uncontrolled division to produce a mass of abnormal cells = 1 (Cancer cells) fail to attach to each other AND spread through the body (to form secondary tumours) = 1	2
2.	(a)		Transcription	1
	(b)		A triplet is a sequence of three nucleotides/bases AND each triplet encodes a specific amino acid	1
	(c)	(i)	DNA strands run from a 3 prime end to a 5 prime end AND in a DNA molecule the strands run in opposite directions	1

Question			Expected Answer(s)	Max mark
		(ii)	(Splice site mutations) can result in introns being left in the primary RNA transcript OR exons being left out of the primary RNA transcript	1
3.	(a)		Missense = 1 Protein/polypetide formed is shorter/contains less amino acids than normal = 1	2
	(b)	(i)	A part of a chromosome is removed AND becomes attached to another chromosome	1
		(ii)	Deletion OR duplication	1
4.	(a)		B A D, E **(both)** C All 4 = 2; 3/2 = 1	2
	(b)		Non-competitive = 1 Inhibitor molecule binds to the enzyme molecule = 1 Changes the shape of the active site = 1	3
5.	(a)	(i)	3.0 mM per litre	1
		(ii)	0.3 mM per litre	1
		(iii)	1.5 mM per litre	1
		(iv)	When activity becomes strenuous more ATP is required and creatine phosphate is broken down to release phosphate and energy for its synthesis = 1 When activity becomes strenuous oxygen becomes deficient in muscle cells some pyruvic acid is converted to lactic acid = 1	2
	(b)	(i)1	Middle distance runner has more/greater % slow twitch AND less/lower % fast twitch OR converse	1
		(i)2	Middle distance runner has less/lower % slow twitch AND more/greater % fast twitch OR converse	1
		(ii)	High % of fast twitch is suitable for the rapid bursts of strenuous activity needed to lift a heavy weight	1
6.	(a)		Progesterone	1
	(b)		Triggers ovulation	1
	(c)		22–26 days	1

Question			Expected Answer(s)	Max mark
	(d)		FSH levels would continue to decrease after day 24 = 1 No further follicle would be developed **AND** no further ova would be released = 1	2
7.	(a)	(i)	She has inherited h from her father (who is X^hY) **AND** from her mother who is a carrier/is X^HX^h/is heterozygous	1
		(ii)	X^HX^h	1
	(b)	(i)	Method to obtain embryonic cells from amniotic fluid before birth (which can be cultured) = 1 Sex chromosomes in karyotype resulting from culture of amniotic cells can be examined before birth = 1	2
		(ii)	100%	1
8.	(a)	(i)	Medulla	1
		(ii)	sympathetic nerve stimulates/speeds heart rate and parasympathetic nerve inhibits/slows heart rate	1
	(b)	(i)	AVN/atrio-ventricular node	1
		(ii)	AVN receives impulses from the SAN = 1 AVN passes impulses down the fibres Y which stimulate contraction of the ventricle walls during ventricular systole = 1	2
9.	(a)		Physical injury **OR** infection **OR** accumulation of LDLs	1
	(b)		Fibrinogen	1
	(c)		Thrombus detaches from the site of thrombosis = 1 Thrombus becomes trapped and blocks a coronary artery = 1	2
10.	(a)	(i)	Insulin caused conversion of glucose to glycogen in the non-diabetic	1
		(ii)	Glucose being released from glycogen by action of glucagon	1
	(b)	1	Usage of glucose in respiration	1
		2	Release of glucose in urine	1
	(c)		In Type 1 the pancreas fails to make insulin In Type 2 the pancreas does not produce enough insulin/liver cells less sensitive to insulin	1

Question			Expected Answer(s)	Max mark
11.			1. Sensory area receives incoming impulses from sense organs 2. Motor area originates impulses to muscles for movement 3. Association areas process information 4. Centres include visual, auditory, language, others **Any 1** 5. Information to and from one side of the body processed by the cerebral hemisphere on the opposite side 6. Transfer of information through the corpus callosum which connects the two hemispheres **Any 3 from points 1–5 AND 1 mark for point 6**	4
12.	(a)	(i)	Insulates fibres **AND** speeds up transmission of impulses	1
		(ii)	Support/nutrition/fighting infection/ production of CS fluid/maintaining a homeostatic environment/removal of debris **Any 1**	1
	(b)	(i)	Vesicle fuses with membrane and releases transmitter into synaptic cleft = 1 Transmitter crosses synapse and binds to receptors in post-synaptic membrane (to pass on impulse) = 1	2
		(ii)	Endorphins	1
13.	(a)		(That increased) caffeine level in blood improves/reduces/has no effect on learning (of motor tasks)	1
	(b)	(i)	Average number of errors per group	1
		(ii)	Diet up to the administration of the experiment Time between taking caffeine and trial External stimuli other than the maze task Maximum time allowed to complete trial Method of administering the caffeine Gender balance/health of individuals **Any 1**	1
	(c)		Repeat the experiment exactly but with another group of ten 25 year old volunteers and no additional caffeine	1
	(d)	(i)	Axes scaled **AND** labelled correctly with units = 1 Points plotted accurately **AND** connected with straight lines = 1 Adding key **OR** labelling lines = 1	3

Question			Expected Answer(s)	Max mark
		(ii)	Not enough individuals tested **OR** not enough trials carried out = **1** Increase sample size **OR** do more trials per individual **OR** repeat tests on individuals = **1**	2
14.	(a)	(i)	91–92 increase from 2800 to 3400 reported cases 92–93 decreased from 3400 to 2600 reported cases 93–96 increased from 2600 to 3600 reported cases **All 3 = 2; 2 = 1**	2
		(ii)	18%	1
	(b)	1	Good hygiene/hand washing following use of toilets **OR** appropriate waste disposal system/quality water supply	1
		2	Good hygiene/hand washing before preparation of food **OR** appropriate storage/handling of food	1
15.	A		1 epithelial cells/skin form a physical barrier 2 epithelial cells produce secretions against infection 3 mast cells produce histamine 4 histamine produces inflammation/vasodilation/capillary permeability/increased blood flow 5 phagocytes/natural killer/NK cells release cytokines which stimulate the specific immune response 6 cytokinins lead to accumulation of phagocytes at infection sites 7 cytokinins lead to delivery of anti-microbial proteins to infection sites 8 cytokinins lead to deleivery of clotting elements to infection sites 9 phagocytes recognise surface antigens on pathogens 10 in phagocytosis pathogens are engulfed/rendered harmless 11 Natural kiler/NK cells induce virally infected cells to undergo apoptosis/produce self-destructive enzymes **Any 8 = 8**	8

Question			Expected Answer(s)	Max mark
	B		1 lymphocytes respond specifically to antigens on foreign cells/pathogens/toxins released by pathogens 2 T lymphocytes have specific surface proteins that allow them to distinguish between body cells and cells with foreign molecules on their surface 3 T lymphocytes induce apoptosis 4 T lymphocytes secrete cytokines which activate B cells and phagocytes 5 B lymphocytes produce specific antibodies 6 antibodies travel in blood and lymph to infected areas 7 antibodies recognise antigens 8 antigen-antibody complexes inactivate pathogens or render them more susceptible to phagocytes 9 antigen-antibody complexes stimulates cell lysis 10 some T and B cells survive as memory cells 11 secondary exposure to antigens results in more rapid and greater immune response **Any 8 = 8**	8

HIGHER FOR CfE HUMAN BIOLOGY MODEL PAPER 2

Section 1

Question	Answer	Mark
1.	D	1
2.	B	1
3.	B	1
4.	C	1
5.	D	1
6.	C	1
7.	A	1
8.	C	1
9.	C	1
10.	B	1
11.	A	1
12.	D	1
13.	A	1
14.	A	1
15.	D	1
16.	B	1
17.	B	1
18.	C	1
19.	D	1
20.	A	1

Section 2

Question			Expected Answer(s)	Max mark
1.	(a)		(Associated) Protein **OR** Histone	1
	(b)		Hydrogen/H	1
	(c)		Thymine	1
	(d)		Antiparallel, phosphate (both)	1
2.	(a)	(i)	41°C	1
		(ii)	Separation of the (DNA) strands/breaking hydrogen bonds between strands/denaturing (of the DNA)	1
		(iii)	They bind/anneal/join to (the ends of the) target/complementary sequences (of DNA being copied).	1
		(iv)	This is closer to the optimum temperature for DNA/taq polymerase.	1
	(b)		Genetic fingerprinting/profiling **OR** amplifying DNA samples from crime scenes **OR** identification of individuals from DNA samples	1

Question			Expected Answer(s)	Max mark
3.			1. Cancer cells have uncontrolled cell division/divide excessively 2. They do not respond to regulatory signals 3. They produce a mass of abnormal cells/which is a tumour 4. They may fail to attach to each other 5. (If they fail to attach to each other) they can spread through the body 6. This can lead to secondary tumours **Any 4**	4
4.	(a)		Oxygen is produced (becoming trapped in the filter paper causing it to float)	1
	(b)	(i)	(Average) time for ten discs to rise	1
		(ii)	Size/surface area/diameter/mass (weight ok)/thickness/type of filter paper/disc **OR** concentration of hydrogen peroxide **OR** height/depth/volume of hydrogen peroxide **OR** height/depth/volume/size/shape/dimensions of beaker **OR** soaking time **OR** temperature of the solution **OR** pH **Any 2, 1 mark each**	2
	(c)		Ten discs were used at each concentration **OR** the experiment was repeated at each concentration **OR** average time was taken for each concentration	1
	(d)		Use discs soaked in water (added to hydrogen peroxide) **OR** Use discs containing no catalase (added to hydrogen peroxide)	1
	(e)		Correct scales, labels and units on axes (average time(s) is acceptable) = 1 Points correctly plotted and line drawn = 1	2
	(f)		1 As (catalase) concentration increases reaction rate/rate of hydrogen peroxide breakdown increases = 1 2 At higher concentrations/above 1% the reaction rate levels off = 1	2
5.	(a)		X glycolysis Y citric acid/TCA/Krebs cycle **Both = 1**	1

Question			Expected Answer(s)	Max mark
	(b)		P oxaloacetate/oxaloacetic acid Q citrate/citric acid **Both = 1**	1
	(c)		Removes hydrogen ions from/electrons from/oxidises substrate **OR** Causes reduction of NAD/FAD/hydrogen acceptor **OR** changes NAD to NADH/FAD to FADH$_2$	1
	(d)	(i)	High energy electrons	1
		(ii)	ATP synthase	1
6.	(a)		24%	1
	(b)		1:3	1
	(c)		The number/% of individuals of high BP increases with age/as they get older **OR** the number of individuals treated increases with age **OR** the number of individuals with normal BP decreases with age. *(Not reference to end result – trend important)* **AND** Long term/accumulated effect of bad diet/smoking/stress/lack of exercise/obesity **OR** lining of the arteries/blood vessels become clogged up/atherosclerosis described **OR** because it is known that older men suffer from high BP, a higher proportion are treated	1
7.	(a)		A = follicle = 1 B = Corpus luteum = 1	2
	(b)		Seminiferous tubule = 1 Sperm production = 1	2
	(c)		Testosterone	1
8.	(a)	(i)	1.8	1
		(ii)	Increase the size of sample/number of women surveyed	1
	(b)		31 million +/−1 million (units necessary)	1
	(c)		3.2	1
	(d)		Mimic negative feedback and inhibit FSH/LH production	1
9.	(a)	(i)	Height and weight/mass	1
		(ii)	30	1
	(b)		Increased energy expenditure **OR** Preserves lean tissue/muscle tissue **OR** Keeps fat content of body low/reduces fat content of body	1

Question			Expected Answer(s)	Max mark
	(c)		Keeps weight/fat/cholesterol under control **OR** Minimises stress **OR** Lowers hypertension/high blood pressure **OR** Improves HDL levels/reduces LDL levels in the blood/improves HDL:LDL ratios **Any 2**	2
10.	(a)		Controls muscles/movement in the right side of the body	1
	(b)		Transfers/shares information/impulses between the two (cerebral) hemispheres/sides of the brain **OR** So brain acts as an integrated whole.	1
	(c)	(i)	The autonomic (nervous system)/ANS	1
		(ii)	Sympathetic speeds it up and parasympathetic slows it down	1
11.	(a)	(i)	Non-aggressive man and girls	1
		(ii)	1770	1
		(iii)	Children will be more aggressive/influenced/likely to copy behaviour/habits if they observe an adult of their own gender/sex (being aggressive) **OR** converse	1
	(b)		Imitation	1
	(c)		Use children who had not seen the recording/adults with the cloth doll Children who had seen recording of cloth doll only	1
12.	(a)		A — diverging/divergent B — converging/convergent **Both = 1**	1
	(b)		Impulses go to many/a number of effectors/muscles/fingers = 1 This allows fine motor control **OR** This allows coordination of the muscles/movements/fingers = 1	2
	(c)		Enzyme breakdown **OR** reabsorption	1
13.	(a)		To allow recognition by the immune system/lymphocytes **OR** so antibodies/memory cells can be produced	1
	(b)		Different strains of flu/the viruses have different antigens/surface proteins/antigenic markers/show antigenic variation.	1

Question		Expected Answer(s)	Max mark
	(c)	1 Destroys infected cells by apoptosis/ production of self-destructive enzymes/inducing suicide = 1 2 Secrete cytokines that activate/ attract B lymphocytes/phagocytes = 1	2
	(d)	It is down to chance which group subjects are placed in/or description of randomised method of allocation to groups eg picking names out of hat = 1 One group receives the vaccine/drug while the other group gets a harmless liquid/dummy drug/the placebo = 1	2
14.	(a)	2005	1
	(b)	25%	1
	(c)	Increase — people becoming complacent about hand washing or bacteria becoming resistant OR No change — everyone now using procedure OR Decrease — increased uptake of procedure	1
	(d)	48	1
	(e)	Clostridium increases Staphylococcus remains fairly constant	1
	(f)	Conclusion — effective = 1 Justification — although percentage of cases remains similar number of cases falls = 1	2

Question			Expected Answer(s)	Max mark
15.	A		1. Ovulation can be stimulated by drugs. 2. These prevent the negative feedback of oestrogen on FSH production. 3. Other drugs/hormones (not FSH/LH) can be given which mimic the action of FSH/LH. 4. These cause super ovulation/the production of a number of ova/ eggs. 5. in vitro fertilisation/IVF programmes. 6. The eggs are removed (surgically) from the ovaries. 7. The eggs are mixed with sperm/ fertilisation occurs outside the body. 8. Fertilised eggs divide/form a ball of cells/at least 8 cells form/form a blastocyst. 9. They are then transferred into the uterus (for implantation). 10. Artificial insemination can be used when the man has a low sperm count. 11. If man is sterile a donor can supply sperm or several samples can be collected from a man with a low sperm count. 12. Intracytoplasmic sperm injection/ ICSI can be used if sperm are defective/low in number. 13. The head of the sperm is injected directly into the egg. **Any 8**	8

Question		Expected Answer(s)	Max mark
B		1. Mother's blood pressure/blood type/blood tests/urine tests/general health check **Any 2**	8
		2. Ultrasound (imaging/scan)	
		3. Dating scan/scan at 8–14 weeks is used to determine stage of pregnancy/due date	
		4. Anomaly scan/scan at 18–20 weeks for serious physical problems	
		5. Biochemical/chemical tests detect (physiological) changes of pregnancy	
		6. Marker chemicals/named chemical can indicate medical conditions/can give a false positive result	
		7. Diagnostic/further testing can follow from routine testing/named test	
		8. Amniocentesis/cells from amniotic fluid used to produce karyotype/to test for Down Syndrome/chromosome abnormalities	
		9. Chorionic villus sampling/CVS — cells from placenta/chorion used to produce karyotype/to test for Down Syndrome/chromosome abnormalities	
		10. CVS carried out earlier in pregnancy than amniocentesis	
		11. Allows immediate karyotyping	
		12. CVS has higher risk of miscarriage	
		13. Rhesus antibody testing described (for sensitisation of Rh-mother by Rh+ antigens). **Any 8**	

HIGHER FOR CfE HUMAN BIOLOGY MODEL PAPER 3

Section 1

Question	Answer	Mark
1.	B	1
2.	C	1
3.	A	1
4.	C	1
5.	D	1
6.	B	1
7.	B	1
8.	D	1
9.	B	1
10.	A	1
11.	C	1
12.	A	1
13.	C	1
14.	B	1
15.	D	1
16.	C	1
17.	A	1
18.	A	1
19.	D	1
20.	D	1

Section 2

Question		Expected Answer(s)	Max mark
1.	(a)	Somatic cells; mitosis Germline cells Meiosis **All 4 = 2; 3/2 = 1**	2
	(b)	Red blood cells Phagocytes/macrophages Lymphocytes Platelets **Any 3 = 2; any 2 = 1**	2
2.	(a)	Peptide = 1 (Mature) mRNA = 1	2
	(b)	arg — tyr — ala — leu **All = 1**	1
	(c)	TGC	1
	(d)	Cutting **AND** combining polypeptide chains **OR** Adding phosphate **OR** Adding carbohydrate **Any = 1**	1

Question			Expected Answer(s)	Max mark
3.	(a)		Glycolysis = 1 Cytoplasm = 1	2
	(b)		Acetyl-CoA	1
	(c)		High concentrations of ATP/citrate inhibit phosphofructokinase	1
	(d)		Releases high energy electrons to the electron transport chain **OR** activates ATP synthase	1
4.	(a)	(i)	Data about DNA sequences which they have in common	1
		(ii)	15	1
	(b)		DNA sequences of patient matched with drug most likely to be beneficial	1
5.	(a)	(i)	As the distance of the event trained for increases, the percentage of slow twitch muscle increases **AND** the percentage of fast twitch muscle decreases	1
		(ii)	3 : 1	1
	(b)		Slow twitch fibres contract more slowly than fast twitch **OR** sustain contractions for longer than fast twitch fibres = 1 Slow twitch have lower glycogen levels than fast twitch **OR** Slow twitch have a higher blood capillary density than fast twitch **OR** Slow twitch have less mitochondria = 1	2
6.	(a)		5%	1
	(b)	(i)	Change in blood pressure	1
		(ii)	Consumption of other drinks/water/ food Activity during trial Age/mass/gender of participants **Any 1**	1
	(c)		Another group not given drink/given 500cm³ plain water (but otherwise treated the in the same way)	1
	(d)		Axes scales and labels = 1 Accurate completion of all four bars = 1	2
	(e)	(i)	The energy drink raises blood pressure	1
		(ii)	Not enough trials/participants	1
	(f)		Double blind = 1 Treatment which does not contain ingredient/material/substance/ chemical/drug being tested = 1	2
7.	(a)	(i)	13.6 µl per ml	1
		(ii)	96.8	1

Question			Expected Answer(s)	Max mark
	(b)		Increases glucose concentration in blood = 1 Glucose needed for respiration to release energy/ATP = 1	2
	(c)		Glycogen	1
	(d)		In type 1 there is no insulin **AND** in type 2 there is insufficient/some insulin/liver cells less sensitive to insulin	1
8.	(a)	(i)	X FSH Z Progesterone **(both)**	1
		(ii)	Ovulation	1
		(iii)	Thickens/repairs endometrium	1
	(b)		Inhibit production of FSH **AND** LH	1
9.	(a)	(i)	Lumen	1
		(ii)	Narrows diameter/cross-section/width Reduces blood flow **Both**	1
	(b)		Clotting factors trigger conversion of prothrombin into thrombin Thrombin causes fibrinogen to be converted into fibrin Fibrin and blood cells form the thrombus/clot All 3 = 2; 2/1 = 1	2
	(c)		Allow vessel to stretch during systole **AND** bounce back/recoil during diastole	1
10.	(a)	(i)	16	1
		(ii)	25%	1
		(iii)	From 0–5 nM increases from 0 to 20 units **AND** From 5–25 nM increases from 20 to 37 units	1
		(iv)	39 units (+/−1)	1
	(b)		2.0 units	1
	(c)		8.5 nM	1
11.	(a)		STM has a limited span/capacity	1
	(b)		Elaboration Rehearsal Organisation **Any 2**	1
	(c)		Related information/meaning from past experience/when information encoded/ memorised (which facilitates retrieval)	1
	(d)		<u>Motor</u> cortex Cortex Limbic system All 3 = 2; 2/1 = 1	2

Question			Expected Answer(s)	Max mark
12.	(a)		Mast cell	1
	(b)		Vasodilation = 1 Increase in capillary permeability = 1	2
	(c)		Cytokines = 1 Accumulation of phagocytes **OR** delivery of anti-microbial protein/clotting elements = 1	2
13.	(a)		Antigens	1
	(b)	(i)	B lymphocyte	1
		(ii)	Only effective against polio antigens OR receptor sites on antibody match the shape of the antigen	1
	(c)		Faster rate of antibody production Longer lasting Greater concentration of antibodies **Any 1**	1
14.			1. Individual responsibility for hygiene 2. Sexual health 3. Storage/handling of food 4. Community responsibility for water quality 5. Safe food webs 6. Waste disposal 7. Vector control **Any 5**	5
15.	A		1. Strands of nucleotides 2. Nucleotide made up of deoxyrobose/sugar, phosphate and base 3. Double helix 4. Sugar-phosphate backbone 5. Complementary base pairing OR A pairs with T and C pairs with G 6. Bases linked by hydrogen bonds 7. Anti-parallel strands 8. 3 prime end has a phosphate AND 5 prime end has a sugar **Any 6** 9. DNA unwinds and unzips/H bond break 10. Primers attach 11. DNA polymerase adds complementary DNA nucleotides 12. Lead strand made continuously 13. Lagging strand made in fragments **OR** ligase joins fragments **Any 3**	9

Question		Expected Answer(s)	Max mark
	B	1. Anabolic pathways require energy 2. Catabolic pathways release energy 3. Reversible and irreversible pathways 4. Regulation by intra and extra cellular molecules 5. Enzymes can work in groups/multi-enzyme complexes 6. Activation energy lowered by enzymes 7. Enzymes have affinity for substrate but less for product molecules 8. Induced fit of enzymes to substrates 9. Fit occurs at active site 10. Enzyme reaction rate can be reduced by inhibitors 11. Competitive inhibitors block active sites 12. Non-competitive inhibitors bind to other regions of enzyme molecule 13. Feedback/end-product inhibition **Any 9**	9

HIGHER FOR CfE HUMAN BIOLOGY 2015

Section 1

Question	Answer	Mark
1.	C	1
2.	C	1
3.	B	1
4.	D	1
5.	D	1
6.	D	1
7.	A	1
8.	D	1
9.	B	1
10.	A	1
11.	B	1
12.	D	1
13.	A	1
14.	A	1
15.	B	1
16.	B	1
17.	A	1
18.	C	1
19.	B	1
20.	C	1

Section 2

Question			Expected Answer(s)	Max mark
1.	(a)		(Relatively) unspecialised (cells) OR Capable of (repeated) division OR Can differentiate (into specialised cells) OR Are totipotent.	1
	(b)		Embryonic stem cells/inner cell mass cells can form all cells types/are totipotent or pluripotent <u>while</u> tissue/adult stem cells can only form a limited range of cell types/are multipotent.	1
	(C)	(i)	Tissue/stem cells are cultured/grown (in laboratory/outside body). OR Tissue/stem cells are transplanted/placed into the muscle/tissue/damaged area.	1
		(ii)	Stem cells can be used to study diseases/cancer. OR Stem cells can be used for <u>drug/medicine</u> testing/treatment.	1

Question			Expected Answer(s)	Max mark
2.	(a)		Anabolic/synthetic/biosynthetic/synthesis	1
	(b)	(i)	It will contain a different <u>nucleotide/base</u>. OR It will contain a different <u>codon</u>/stop <u>codon</u>.	1
		(ii)	The protein/enzyme/glycogen synthase contains a different <u>amino acid(s)</u>.	1
	(c)		Glucose is used up in respiration/to provide energy/ATP <u>and</u> they have no <u>glycogen</u> stores to provide more glucose.	1
	(d)		*Recessive* Disease skips generations/does not appear in every generation. OR Two unaffected/heterozygous/carrier parents can have an affected child.　*1 mark* *Sex-linked* **More males** will be affected than females. OR **Affected males** do not pass the allele/condition to their sons. OR **Affected males** can <u>only</u> pass the allele/condition to their daughters. OR **Unaffected males** cannot pass the allele/condition to their daughters. OR Only **affected/carrier females** pass the condition to their sons.　*1 mark*	2
3.	(a)		• Volume of yeast suspension/solution/cells. • Concentration of yeast suspension/solution/ number of yeast cells/mass of yeast. • Type/age/source of yeast cells. • Area/size/diameter/volume/thickness/type of gel or dish. • Concentration of nutrients in gel/pH of gel. • Strength or intensity of lamp/use same lamp/distance of lamp. • Temperature of incubator/dishes. • Time for yeast to grow/dishes left in incubator.　*Any two*	2
	(b)	(i)	Axes have correct scales and labels　*1 mark* Points correctly plotted and line drawn (touching each point).　*1 mark*	2
		(ii)	Increasing the exposure (to UV radiation) <u>increases</u> the number of yeast cells/colonies that <u>die</u>/are <u>damaged</u>. OR Increasing the exposure (to UV radiation) <u>decreases</u> the number of yeast cells/colonies that <u>survive</u>.	1

Question			Expected Answer(s)	Max mark
		(iii)	Repeat the investigation <u>at each exposure</u> (time). **OR** Repeat the investigation and calculate <u>averages</u>.	1
	(c)	(i)	400	1
		(ii)	The number of yeast cells/colonies at SPF 15 is almost as much as with higher SPF values. **OR** There are more yeast cells/colonies using SPF 15 compared to when using no sunscreen.	1
		(iii)	350 minutes/5 hours 50 minutes	1
4.	(a)		ATP is broken down/used up/converted to ADP. **OR** ATP is put into the reaction.	1
	(b)		It changes the shape/form of the active site (to suit the substrate molecule). **OR** It induces a better fit with the substrate. **OR** It <u>lowers</u> the activation energy.	1
	(c)		Enzyme 1 **OR** Enzyme 3 Explanation: The transfer of phosphate/addition of phosphate (from ATP)	1
	(d)		When there has been a build-up/too much/an increased concentration of <u>fructose-6-phosphate</u>.	1
	(e)		This ensures the cell only <u>produces ATP</u> when required **OR** This ensures that <u>glucose is only used</u> when it is required/conserved.	1
5.	(a)	(i)	Releases/supplies <u>energy</u> (rapidly/at a fast rate). *1 mark* <u>Phosphate</u> (released) is used to convert ADP to ATP/to create ATP. *1 mark*	2
		(ii)	The creatine phosphate supply runs out (after 10 seconds).	1
	(b)		Lactic acid/lactate.	1

Question			Expected Answer(s)	Max mark
	(c)		Muscle fibre: Slow twitch Sport: any suitable endurance sport Reasons: • they contract (relatively) slowly • can contract over a (relatively) long period • have many mitochondria • have a large blood supply • rely on aerobic respiration (to generate ATP) • have a high concentration of myoglobin • stores/energy source is mainly fat. Muscle fibre: Fast twitch Sport: any sport requiring bursts of energy Reasons: • they contract (relatively) quickly • can contract over a (relatively) short period • have few mitochondria • have a low blood supply • rely on glycolysis (to generate ATP) • have a low concentration of myoglobin • stores/main energy source is glycogen/creatine phosphate. *Any 3 reasons for 3 marks*	3
6.	(a)	(i)	Cross (centre) is placed in the fetal tissue area.	1
		(ii)	Cells are cultured/allowed to divide (to obtain sufficient cells) *1 mark* (Karyotypes then show) the <u>chromosomes</u> (from the cells). *1 mark*	2
		(iii)	CVS can be carried out earlier (in pregnancy than amniocentesis).	1
	(b)		Biochemical	1
7.	(a)		18	1
	(b)		(As children get older) they eat less 'healthy' food/have a higher fat diet/have more sugar in their diet. **OR** (As children get older) they choose/control what they eat. **OR** (As children get older) they exercise less/carry out less physical activities.	1
	(c)		Weight divided by height <u>squared</u>.	1

Question			Expected Answer(s)	Max mark
	(d)		Identification — use celebrities/role models/someone they admire to promote a healthy lifestyle/healthy diet/exercise. *1 mark* Internalisation — Use adverts/media/parents/reasoned arguments/persuasion to get children to adopt a healthy lifestyle/healthy diet/exercise. *1 mark*	2
8.	(a)		Between work levels 1 to 5 the stroke volume increased <u>and</u> then it remained constant between levels 5 and 7. *1 mark* It increased from 88 cm^3 to 140 cm^3 **OR** it remained constant at 140 cm^3. *1 mark*	2
	(b)		102	1
	(c)		19 600	1
	(d)	(i)	4·5	1
		(ii)	120 beats/min	1
		(iii)	23·81/23·8/24	1
9.	(a)		<u>Enough/increased/more/a higher concentration</u> of <u>dopamine/neurotransmitter</u> (is released) to trigger an impulse/reach threshold. **OR** <u>Many/a series</u> of <u>weak stimuli</u> trigger an impulse/reach threshold.	1
	(b)		Provides <u>energy/ATP</u> to make/release neurotransmitter or dopamine/form vesicles/allow vesicles to move/allow vesicles to fuse with the membrane/to reuptake neurotransmitter.	1
	(c)		(Cocaine) blocks/inhibits/acts as an antagonist to the re-uptake <u>proteins</u>. **OR** (Cocaine) prevents the <u>proteins</u> from reabsorbing/taking up/removing dopamine. *1 mark* Dopamine/neurotransmitter remains in the synapse/at the receptors. **OR** Dopamine/neurotransmitter continues to stimulate receptors/fire impulses. *1 mark*	2

Question			Expected Answer(s)	Max mark
10.	(a)		Organisation Related information is grouped together. **OR** Information is put into categories/headings. *1 mark* Elaboration Additional information is given (about each term). **OR** Meaningful information is given (about each term). *1 mark*	2
	(b)		<u>Short-term</u> memory/STM has a limited capacity/span/only holds around 7 items of information.	1
	(c)		Cerebrum/cortex	1
11.	(a)	(i)	Release histamine *1 mark* This causes vasodilation/increased <u>capillary</u> permeability *1 mark* **OR** Release cytokines *1 mark* This leads to an accumulation of phagocytes/the delivery of antimicrobial proteins/clotting elements *1 mark*	2
		(ii)	NK cells induce/cause the <u>infected/invaded cell</u> to self-destruct/undergo apoptosis/undergo programmed cell death. *1 mark*	1
	(b)		Phagocytes engulf/capture/digest the bacteria/pathogen. *1 mark* They display the bacteria's/pathogen's <u>antigens</u> on their surface (activating T-lymphocytes). *1 mark*	2
12.	(a)		26 million/26 000 000	1
	(b)		0·6 million/600 000	1
	(c)		5·14/5·1/5	1
	(d)		The steep<u>est</u>/steep<u>er</u> part of the (HIV infected) graph/line was between 1993 and 1995 **OR** The graph/line <u>sharply increases</u> between 1993 and 1995 while the rest of the graph/line <u>more steadily</u> increases.	1

Question			Expected Answer(s)	Max mark
13.	(a)	(i)	Each group should contain individuals of similar ages/a similar age range. **OR** Each group should contain the same number of males and females/same gender mix. **OR** Individuals in groups should have no recent history of influenza. **OR** Individuals should not be allowed to travel abroad during the study **OR** Individuals should all be in good general health.	1
		(ii)	Did not develop influenza = 453 <u>and</u> Total = 470	1
		(iii)	R	1
	(b)		It enhances/improves the immune response/antibody production. **OR** It improves the <u>effectiveness</u> of the vaccine.	1
	(c)		A pandemic	1
14.	(a)	(i)	1. Pituitary gland secretes/produces FSH/LH. 2. FSH stimulates growth of <u>follicle</u> (in the ovary). 3. Follicle/ovary produces oestrogen. 4. Oestrogen stimulates growth/repair/proliferation/thickening of endometrium/uterus lining. 5. Oestrogen stimulates production of LH. 6. LH (surge) brings about ovulation/release of the egg. 7. <u>Rising/high levels</u> of oestrogen inhibit FSH production. 8. This is negative feedback *Any 6 points for 6 marks*	6

Question			Expected Answer(s)	Max mark
		(ii)	a. The follicle develops into the corpus luteum. b. Corpus luteum secretes progesterone (and oestrogen). c. Progesterone maintains/increases/thickens the endometrium/uterus lining. d. Progesterone inhibits <u>FSH/LH</u> production. e. Progesterone/oestrogen levels decrease (towards the end of the cycle). f. This/corpus luteum degeneration triggers menstruation/breakdown of the endometrium. *Any 4 points for 4 marks*	4
	(b)	(i)	1. Pacemaker/SAN contains autorhythmic cells/is where the heart beat originates/is found in the right atrium. 2. <u>Impulse/wave of excitation</u> spreads across the atria/cause the atria to contract/cause atrial systole. 3. (Impulses) reach/stimulate the atrioventricular node/AVN. 4. AVN found at junction of atria and ventricles/at base of atria. 5. Impulses from AVN spread through ventricles. 6. (Cause) contraction of ventricles/ventricular systole. 7. (This is followed by) relaxation/resting/diastolic phase/diastole. *Any 5 points for 5 marks*	5
		(ii)	a. <u>Medulla</u> controls the cardiac cycle/regulates the SAN. b. <u>Autonomic nervous system</u> (carries impulses to heart). c. <u>Sympathetic</u> nerve speeds up the heart rate. d. Sympathetic nerve releases noradrenaline/norepinephrine. e. <u>Parasympathetic</u> nerve slows down the heart rate. f. Parasympathetic nerve releases acetylcholine. g. Sympathetic and parasympathetic systems are <u>antagonistic</u> to each other *Any 5 points for 5 marks*	5